T0208953

Reawaken
The Spirit Warrior

A Path To Becoming Reawakened
& Unleashing Your Awesome

RITA ALDO RASI

BALBOA.PRESS
A DIVISION OF HAY HOUSE

Copyright © 2019 Rita Aldo Rasi.

All rights reserved. No part of this book may be used or reproduced by
any means, graphic, electronic, or mechanical, including photocopying,
recording, taping or by any information storage retrieval system
without the written permission of the author except in the case of
brief quotations embodied in critical articles and reviews.

Balboa Press books may be ordered through booksellers or by contacting:

Balboa Press
A Division of Hay House
1663 Liberty Drive
Bloomington, IN 47403
www.balboapress.com
1 (877) 407-4847

Because of the dynamic nature of the Internet, any web addresses or
links contained in this book may have changed since publication and
may no longer be valid. The views expressed in this work are solely those
of the author and do not necessarily reflect the views of the publisher,
and the publisher hereby disclaims any responsibility for them.

The author of this book does not dispense medical advice or prescribe the use
of any technique as a form of treatment for physical, emotional, or medical
problems without the advice of a physician, either directly or indirectly. The
intent of the author is only to offer information of a general nature to help
you in your quest for emotional and spiritual well-being. In the event you use
any of the information in this book for yourself, which is your constitutional
right, the author and the publisher assume no responsibility for your actions.

Any people depicted in stock imagery provided by Getty Images are
models, and such images are being used for illustrative purposes only.
Certain stock imagery © Getty Images.

Print information available on the last page.

ISBN: 978-1-9822-3943-5 (sc)
ISBN: 978-1-9822-3945-9 (hc)
ISBN: 978-1-9822-3944-2 (e)

Library of Congress Control Number: 2019919658

Balboa Press rev. date: 11/29/2019

This Book is Dedicated to the Readers.

For those of you who felt compelled to pick this book up with a yearning to learn something you don't quite understand. For those with a sense of knowing yet unknowing all at the same time. For those of you who feel that there is more than what society outlines and the reality that is right in front of you. Those who feel drawn to learn more, yearn to be more... to be the best you can be, to become reawakened. For those who are now reawakening and yearn for the path to unfold before them.

I wrote this book during my own journey to becoming reawakened and in the process of re-claiming myself, revising my path, reawakening my inner spirit, reclaiming my heart and re-igniting my soul. I don't claim to be a master, or guru or teacher. I am merely a student, and a person that felt compelled to write this process during my own journey.

Truthfully, I embraced each moment, I claimed all of my tears, learned from each of the lessons. I uncovered my fears one by one and savored each moment thru the passion written on these pages. I pray that you identify with my words, my journey and become enlightened by your own path and the exciting journey you are embarking upon.

This now is your journey, your pursuit of what you want to learn, and your process of relearning. My hope is that you allow my words to propel some deep thought, some potent action and the steps to becoming a better version of you.

Embrace the thought process, the nuances and above all enjoy the journey!

Spiritual awareness brings strength to the
heart and confidence to the mind.
It nourishes and expands, becoming the solid
anchor during the worst of storms,
And the beacon of light that shines throughout your life.
~ Rita Aldo Rasi

Prelude

With my hands held up high, palms facing up to the heavens, and my eyes closed. I could feel the tears rushing down my face with such a rapid frenzy, yet peacefully free flowing as they tricked down my face, then to my chin and speckled my clothes as they fell downwards in a parade of freedom free fall. I could feel this tremendous release with each tear allowing all of the pain, heartache and sorrow, exit through my entire body and extremities. I found my body swaying to the music deeply immersed, in the collective movement rushing over the 300+ people around me, in a sort of rhythmic soulful dance. I could feel my whole body changing at this very moment, from my insides, my cells on a micro and macro level. It was like the transformation happened within moments, yet the Divine had a plan for me and little did I know that this change was in process for years, I merely realized it as it unfolded before me.

Each and everyone of us in the theatre was experiencing their own individual transformation and spiritual cleansing, varied by their own past stories, yet united in this collective releasing bath. My tears flowing steady now, and my voice also found its way to sing this slow, yet profound unknown song, growing stronger and stronger with each verse. The strength in my voice surprised even myself, with its robust sound and flow of its words.

RA…..MA…..DA….SA………SA….   SAY……. SO…….. HUNG…..

In this very moment I felt my footing solid on my path, I knew this is where I was supposed to be. But how did I get here? How did I find myself in a cozy dark rich theatre on 52nd street, in downtown Manhattan in New York City, with 300+ other people I have never met before, at the very first Spirit Masterclass with Gabby Bernstein. Yet I felt so at home, amongst 300 strangers, I felt each one as my fellow brothers and sisters. We bonded thru song, thru our tears, our sorrow, our release and our call to the Divine. Then a most angelic voice rang thru the arches of this beautiful theatre…………. I am thine…………. I… am….. I could simply feel my breath and my pulse hold as this song rang thru this old building and echoed with such grace. I was filled with such happiness and oneness as her voice seems to surround each and everyone of us like a warm long-awaited hug. I was to embrace this new change, yet I would be ok. I would later realise that this song and angelic voice came from world renown singer Jai Jagdeesh, who I would later have the absolute pleasure of meeting in person. Oh, how her song radiated thru my body. I could see her song affecting each and everyone of us. I found myself at peace, and in flow with my mind, my body and my soul. It was like all the pieces finally came together yet, I knew this feeling before. I had felt it many, many years ago as a young girl. This fully tranquil feeling of being home. Soulfully aware of the essence my being, the longing of my heart and the trueness of my soul. I felt free and tranquil as if I could reach the heavens. It had been years since I felt this type of serenity and peacefulness and thought of a time years ago when I was 12 years old, in a small round ornate church in Pisa Italy. I recalled the song of a priest and a small collection of nuns, singing that echoed thru the church halls that slowly engulfed its every room and its golden dome. It touched my heart and resonated in my soul for years, which I can remember at a moment's notice. This deep feeling of complete acceptance and happiness that radiated thru out my entire body. This was it! I could feel the same oneness and craved for more, much much more, but my mind was racing. How did I find myself here? After all of these years, how did I get here so many years later. So unannounced, so unguided, and undetermined. This was so divinely executed…. I sat down and realized that I had been on the journey unwittingly for years. My soul had craved to go back to this divine place of peace and soulful knowing, but I had not been willing to engage for many years thinking I knew what was best. That I was in control and it was up to me to properly navigate my path.

My spiritual journey really took flight unbeknownst to me, years earlier on the top-level floor of the Indigo Chapters store at Yorkdale Mall in Toronto Ontario. I had just had a pretty intense meeting with my financial advisor and was wandering the store in a trance reviewing all of the elements of my life that had culminated into my current financial situation. We have all pondered our situations and how we were lead to our current status and I was no different. Being a single mom, with two kids in university, a mortgaged home, working full time, side part-time work, my immediate family sick with major diseases, and a fledgling side hustle-business, I found myself in the Self-Help Section looking for inspiration. Yes, secretly hoping for that incredible miracle that would impact my life. Oh, how I had prayed and asked for some divine guidance… All I wanted was that secret slice of knowledge, that golden nugget, I didn't know existed. Well little did I know, what the universe had in store for me. For it had heard my calls, and was primed and ready for action. For those who knew me then, knew that this was not a typical section I would frequent, let alone spent much time in. However, in saying that, since I found myself lingering, I was called to look for a book I had been suggested to read by famous author Victor Frankel – The Meaning of Man. I had been told it was an amazing book that I just had to read. (Amazing book, right?) Well I digress, I found the book, and was browsing thru as we all do, and after a few moments of perusing, I was stunned to have a hard cover book hit me on the side of the head from a higher shelf completely out of the blue. Now one would wonder, why no nasty obscenities didn't come flying out of my mouth, but in reality, who would believe me? Also, there truly was no one around me to yell at. The older man in the same isle who was about 8 feet from me, lowered his black rimmed glasses, and looked at me in disbelief and stated" Hey I think you may need to buy that book"! To which I replied "Hmmm ya no Shit!!", as I rubbed the side of my head. Now weird shit has always seemed to happened to me or around me, but this was definitely a first. Nothing like a hard inadament object literally hitting me in the head. If someone really wanted my attention, well they definitely had it! So, as I gathered the book from the floor and continued to rub my dented head, I noticed that the book had a cute blonde lady on the front wearing a sequin dress and a happy face on the front. Wow, just what I needed I thought, a happy hippy blonde chick with a happy glittery life. Just what I needed, now how on earth can this help me? I mean really?? The book was *Spirit Junkie by Gabrielle Bernstein*. Never heard of her, but man she must have some fantastic marketing people if she can make books hit you in the head, just to get your attention! Clearly, on a subconscious level, I knew I was meant to pick this book up and have a look as we all know we really should not test the universe. To be honest, after noting on what good aim the Universe had already demonstrated, I wasn't really willing to risk my chances again, after all I did ask......

I put down my Victor Frankel book for this Junkie book. Needless to say, I had already read past the second chapter by the time I reached the front cashier, not even wondering how and if I could afford to pay for it. I was hooked, Gabrielle's book had not only woken me up but had unknowingly set me on my path of becoming reawakened. I didn't know this at the time, but I was well on my way to a spiritual journey I could have never estimated nor imagined. No one truly asks to be on a spiritual journey, but mine was at a pivotal time when I just knew and understood that this was destined, to create change in my life. I was all consumed, and I finished the book understanding the lessons and expanded my thought process to place I never knew existed. I was then fortunate enough to meet Gabby later on the following year at her very first Masterclass Summit-Level One in NYC and 6 months later in her first Level Two Masterclass in Stockbridge, Mass. Along with Rah Goddess, Kris Carr, and Gala Darling.

Thus, allowing me, to not only learn from great spiritual masters that taught me expansive lessons and rituals, but preparing me for a higher learning, and gifting me an amazing network of like-minded light workers. Within months, I had unknowingly found my tribe, my spiritual peers and also realised that Gabby's hard-hitting book had been knocking over many people all over the world. How very creative, and what a marketing genius! Joking aside, the universe had other plans for me and was forcing me to realign my thoughts, my path and my mission in life. Showing me a path along with many other like-minded souls to become more conscious on how we live, how we treat each other, how to collectively shine our passions to the greater good and how we live our truth. Here I was worried about my finances, the extra weight I gained, and other materialistic things, that had driven my life for many years. I found later to be so meaningless, yet the divine source other plans for me all along. Most of us are never sure nor clear on what we have been brought here to do. Some are called to serve eagerly and some of us are completely scared shitless. I myself had always known there was more to life, but had asked for clarity. Never realizing how a simple book, or thought process could have truly transform me, my soul and my life.

My sub-conscious had become awakened and had begun to see more clearly a life in which I lived in a completely different light. Whether we choose it or not, the Universe always has your back (check out Gabby's new book Universe has your back") and it will conspire to give you what you want and need. I had asked for clarity for years, for a clear vision that was my own. My own passion and mission on this planet. I felt like I was brought to be of service. The fact that there was more to this life than just working, sleeping and paying taxes… The Divine, the universe, God, Allah, or whatever you call your higher power knows us, hears us and answers us.

We just need to be willing to hear and pay attention, to truly listen without condition or judgement. In essence, don't ask for help if you don't truly want the help or direction because you never know what will happen. All I can say is that if you crave something more and truly want direction, all you simply have to do is ask. Your answer will appear. I just say be ready. You need to be truly ready for what may come your way. What answers or what direction you will be given.

Give of yourself freely and with free abandon for what the universe has in store for you. Some of us literally need to be hit in the head, while others may seek it out. Regardless of the circumstance it is your own narrative that we are able to write or rewrite. Be willing to learn, be I truly hope you will find your path, easily and freely and are given some true signs like my book, that will hopefully guide you and allow you to walk confidently in your journey, for the Divine, will plan always plan amazing things for us, all in good time. For myself I can say....

Thank you, universe for grabbing my attention.........

The Era of Re

*M*ost people base their identity with their name, last name or on their race, their culture and/or their religion. Thus, rooting yourself from a distinct route of origin. For myself my name never truly aligned with me, and I was never given a middle name so I always felt somewhat undefined. I never knew a lot of Rita's until College and found it was not a typical Italian name. Silly yes, but in itself Rita for me was too short, too non-descript and not a true expression or description of myself, or my potential. I didn't fit in. I didn't look nor act like the rest of my family and my name was the same. Everyone had a strong first name and conjoining middle name. So, you may ask, what did I expect my name to describe? Well a sense of me I guess, a sense of my origin, my culture, or a direct result of my family... something. I wasn't named after anyone, like many others in my family, so I felt so un-defined and perhaps unimportant. This bothered me for many, many years...... and simply never felt part of something larger or definite. Yet, as I unknowingly begun my spiritual path to becoming reawakened, I realized that the un-descript name was exactly who and what I was. The un-determined and non-descript name I was Ri (as my friends call me) in the process of becoming Reawakened, it was in that process that I was in the right place at the right time to Reflect, Release, Reclaim and in itself become Reawakened. The textbook origins of **re**-a word-forming element meaning "back to the original place; again, anew, once more," also with a sense of "undoing," c.1200, from Old French and directly from Latin *re*-"again, back, anew, against," How fitting that my journey to re-kindle my spirit, and to re-new my path, and re-learn all that this world has taught me, that I am becoming re-awakened... I entered into the era of Re.... You see, I believe that we have all been here to learn, to re-learn, re-identify, and re-calibrate our thought process and the stories and belief systems we are taught to live by.

My path is my own journey, my process, my mistakes, and ultimately my life with many detours that are all my own that each cultivated its own lessons. You see, reawakening is a process of breaking, learning, relearning and mending. Each break causes ripple effects to all aspects of your life, your mind and soul thus allowing the light to come in..... amongst the darkness of the trauma each lesson caused in its wake.

My true hope is that this book will give you methods to use along your path, give you reasons and explanations to your wondering, some rituals help along your journey, some answers to your questions, some books for your learning, and some music to your yearning ears. Your path is your very own, drive at your own pace, pack your tool box, take in the scenery, stop along the way, or when you feel the need, reassess, realign and enjoy! Embrace each and every experience, learn from the lessons, take notes, and happily thank those you meet on your way. Regardless, of what good or bad may come your way, remember that you must embrace each in itself as it brings you their lessons.

Allow the universe to guide you on your journey.

Safe travels!

Contents

Era One

Re-awakening............ the reason,
the route, the result

Re a·wak·en ing (ə-wā′kən). a·wak·ened, a·wak·en·ing, a·wak·ens

1. To wake up again:
2. To become aware of something again:
3. To cause (someone) to become aware; alert or enlighten:
4. To stir up or produce (a memory or feeling, for example):

Re-awakening............ the reason, the result, the route.

*W*ell let me start by saying, that no one is going to sit you in a comfy chair and offer you a blue or red pill. This is no guided tour nor are there leaders who think you're the "one". No rabbit hole or lady in a red dress to let you know you're in the matrix or a mad hatter to tell you what time it is. LOL...... Seriously, no one will openly volunteer a comfortable chair and share an explanation of what is happening to you and exactly what will occur with absolute certainty. A spiritual awakening or re-awakening as I call it, is different for everyone and varies with the narrative backpack that each of us brings around with us. Our paths vary as different as the stories we have lived by. Each path is the system or process to unravel the programed belief system given to us during our lives, by our parents, our families, upbringing, culture, religion and support systems. This story is firmly based on our past beliefs, painful experiences, successes and failures that give us the framework of what we call our inner stories. This is what we hold dear and ideally sets the foundation of all other decisions, are made from and what we live by.

For years many elders would reclaim their religion, or possibly look into another vein of religion to seek a better understand of life as we call it. This rite of passage, as we all seek a better understanding as we inevitably edge closer to the end of our life span, or departure here on earth. In this time, you would find your parents, grandparents or great grandparents spending more and more time in prayer, in deep thought or at their place of worship. This bringing mindfulness, introspective thought and often an intricate review of their life, regrets and accomplishments. This was also coupled with much quiet time of reflective thoughts on the life they had lived, and more importantly things that were never completed or a life truly lived. As we each seek a greater understanding of our lives and our time here on earth, we unwittingly always tend to review our purpose in this life and promotes the thought process to ask more profound questions.

Today, spirituality has been increasing in popularity to not only evaluate everything from our lives, our religion and the pursuit of spirituality but as it fits best for the individual. Spirituality you see, signifies something completely different to each of us, depending on what your needs are. For some a more in-depth assessment is required allowing each of us to delve deeper into our own thought process and challenge our belief systems with a new understanding of the world we currently live in. With all facts formerly known, that built the foundation of our belief systems now converts to a fresh perspective in a new understanding. In essence, we are all spiritual beings having a human experience, so while we each try our best to navigate our way thru successfully, we all have different obstacles to work around or thru.

Remember our narrative can be changed or revised at any time so when we all decide to spend time in deep thought of our past stories is thoroughly dependent on you. This brings us to the reason of a reawakening.

The Reason

_I_ believe that each and every one of us were born for a higher purpose. We have dreams that have selected us and, in our life, it is our path and our duty to find that purpose and passion. Although some of us find our purpose or reason early on, yet some of us find our direction later in our life due to our path to unlearning, and resistance to hearing your calling. No one version is better nor worse, yet each is important in its own way. What I have come to realize is that those who reawaken early, navigate very differently than those who reawaken later in life. Remember we live with our inner stories for years, releasing these stories or inner beliefs much like peeling an onion. Each layer is filled with a life filled with experiences, stories and belief systems that influence each and every day, this assists us to navigate. So, by peeling back each layer allows us to reveal, review and ideally understand why and how we are who we are. You see we come to be taught and in this our parents teach us a version of their conditioning. This is what assists to mold us into the people we become with fears, interests, thoughts, likes and dislikes. What makes us tick and how and why do we react the way that we do, even though we know the correct behaviors. In the end, we are all spiritual beings, living a human existence, processing and dealing with life best way we can. It is in this life that we are to live, learn and comprehend the lessons we are meant to acquire here on earth.

Have you ever see someone who just seems to know what career they want, and simply follow it without hesitation? Yet some others seem to roam aimlessly for years trying to find their niche in life? The only thing that separates those two is the understanding of what they need to do. It does not mean one is greater than the other, or that one is smarter or more determined. The understanding and navigation is all part of this process as complex and simple as it needs to be. The reason of a spiritual reawakening is the same and is not partial to those who have or who don't have a claimed religion. The process of reawakening is so very personal, its intimate in nature and so highly sacred to those navigating this path. I personally believe that each and every one of us have been brought here for a reason and some of us have been brought here before. As children we were born awakened with a freedom to love freely, to openly appreciate beauty, to openly experience and appreciate joy and to fully embrace happiness by living in the moment in all aspects of our lives. Ever notice how in love a child can be with a movie, a type of ice cream or their favorite treat? They love openly and freely without hesitation and without restriction. I feel that during our lives we are then taught to put aside these open emotions and shelter our feelings and inner thoughts to shield ourselves. To reopen this type of thought process is to reawaken these true feelings and belief. The signs of spiritual awakening for most comes as a surprise until the realization of what is actually happening.

To some, it could be a hindrance as in some cases that will cause you to slow you down in the everyday things that you do. It makes you crave solitude, or reflective time in which to read, write and possible reflect on all things past coupled with thoughts of the future and your place within it. You will crave things you never gave a second thought to think about let alone participate in. In some cases, it may also force thoughts of past issues that you were not ready or prepared to truly look at or deal with head on. This in itself causes a new inner dialogue that makes us renew our will for change and seek a new understanding and thought process. Some feel a few days of being reclusive and others may be forced into bed to complete processes these feelings. This would not be your usual "sick days" but alas this just as required as when you are taking some down time from a cold. If you are anything like myself, then you may spend weeks, months or years resisting your spiritual awakening symptoms. It is not for the faint hearted.... Our awareness is often muddled with the urgency of everyday occurrences and an unknowing of what these symptoms or thoughts are. For some signs of signs of spiritual reawakening have been playing out for years with many thoughts playing out subconsciously or within conversations with others that become a Deja vu in a sort of knowing. Like myself I had always had different experiences but was always taught that this was not to be discussed. My conditioning and belief system had always held me from truly hearing the call I was so desperately asking the universe for. Silly no? Well it isn't until you truly allow the layers to be peeled back and that you start allowing your old thought patterns to unravel that you begin to see more clearly. Like wiping off a haze from your glasses, you not only see, but hear and understand things with more clarity and a profound understand that was never possible before. Most would ask, how can this be? How can you change how you see and view things within days of each other? Well although I agree and found the whole concept a bit odd at first, remember we each process things differently and no one way is incorrect or wrong. The reason we change is different for all. It's like listening to a song on the radio that you have heard so many times before, yet the words suddenly take on a more valid and correct meaning. The beat is the same, but you seem to notice and understand more hidden meaning from before. Like an upgraded program or phone, your ability to process is heightened. What is the result you ask? Great question.

The Result

This process of knowing is a slow process that reveals and transforms different layers of your energy body that's held you in one place. When these layers are released, you expand. So, with each layer you expand and evolve to a point where you are evolving faster and faster causing you to feel overwhelmed and tired more quickly. In time some become strong enough to transmute heavy layers underneath which until you were ready, remained hidden.

This process of revealing and transforming is what results in the signs of spiritual awakening. This takes years and much understanding. There is a purpose to it all and in time, the symptoms will ease and your feeling of expansion will last longer resulting in a higher understanding and view of the world. Things that one day would make your blood boil now gives you an even resolve that seems natural. Many around you may feel you have changed your mind and would simply not understand and that's ok! It is all due part of the process. This expansion of thoughts and understanding allows for varied views of hurt, anger, and resentment resolve to change in a state of understanding without judgement.

As you navigate thru this, you will find that issues that used to cause elevated anxiety and hurt and anger would now allow a differed thought process to view the issue in another view point thus gathering a different understanding of the situation, the people involved and perhaps even what caused the events to process as they did which was not seen before. Why is this important? Well as humans we are wired to learn, to understand and to emotionally feel connected. Although certain decisions and emotions can separate and divide us it can also allow us to further evolve to understand and expand our thought process. It has been stated that there is a very fine line between love and hate. What also needs to be elaborated on is that thru learning as humans we can evolve to better understand our deepest thoughts of hatred and to passionate love. This allows us to question why and what causes us to reach such deep and high emotions. Once we can pass thru the emotion it gives us the opportunity to review each issue that is given to us as a lesson to learn and expand on. Yes, I know some issues you really want to question. What the hell, why did I need to go thru that? Or my favorite is always. Why, does this keep happening to me? Oh, the amount of times I said that. I vividly remember a time when I expressed that very sentence. As I loomed in my air of disbelief on how undeserving I was that the universe had given me the proverbial short stick. When an amazing and dear friend (Wanda) I will never forget… humbly and softly stated.

"Well sweetie, it's because you haven't learned the lesson yet." WTF? How many times, did I need to go thru the same pain and emotional ringer for me to learn? Was I just not getting it? Am I attracting the same situation? What was I missing? Did I miss the memo? Did I need to read a book? Why was I not reaching or learning the lessons? I wanted off of the hamster wheel and wanted to learn and expand... quickly. Oh, my dear friend Wanda knew so much more than I did at that time. If I only knew what was in store for me! So I asked the question…. (thank you Wanda!) Did you hear me universe? I want to learn. Show me! Well if only I could have seen the answer readily, I would have easily realized that like Dorothy from the Wizard of Oz that I had my red shoes and I had the power all along.

All I needed to do was to look out from my pain, and to allow myself to fully comprehend the problem, the solution and the people in play and how each of us had our own version of the truth. Wow what a concept! Oh, the years of therapy I could have a refund for! ☺ Well joking aside, at this time, you may choose to keep your "new resolve" to yourself as your energy body expands, and although you know that you may make great leaps, feel on top of the world, this too can be met with a time to regress for a time. Each is part of the process and as one issue is completed another may come forward, or some will come back to resolve further. Remember it is best for us to navigate at our own pace. There is no rush to the finish line, so there is no right and wrong. We each navigate our way thru this maze to the best of our abilities. Never fret we all need down time and sometimes have to make a hard stop to review and reprocess again.

The Route

*W*ell there is no map to this destination nor can this be found on MapQuest, or on your GPS. I personally had issues with this from time to time debating if my thought process and choices were correct. All I can say here is that you always need to do what feels right. Our inner compass will always guide us to our re-awakening. We can each find our path to become re-awakened at different times in our lives and by very different causes, but ideally for all, for the same reason. For some, it hits them like they have been put into another universe, with a complete new vision and insight, or to have just walked into a scene for the Matrix (one of my favorite movies!!!) with everything they ever knew now had a new meaning, along with a feeling of unknowing why. For others it was a fruition of many hints, signs and guidance that finally comes to light. It is in this pregnant moment that gives us each a new meaning to life yet varies with each and every one of us.

Having spoken to, many in my community, I can firmly say that many can explain and describe the subtle signs and moments that propelled them to this new understanding. It's like watching a movie and then someone explains all of the subtle nuances that completely change your perspective you had original rendered. In essence, we each have our own narrative that we can rewrite, with a new understanding and acceptance. It is said that those who seek a higher learning, or a better understanding seem to evolve more quickly and reach within into their deep sub-conscious. This level of understanding and dedication that there is indeed more to life than merely working, paying bills, paying taxes, acquiring degrees of wealth, raising a family and dying is not a new concept. It is the age, old question of what are we here for?

In the reawakening process, you actually want and yearn for the answer, seek the reasons for the answer and want to grow, to expand, to learn and fully comprehend rather than just ask a rhetorical question to sound smart. We are all here to learn but need to look at where the lessons and learning comes from with more intensity and scrutiny. What we have come to understand is set for us to learn is not a learning environment but yet more conditioning to induce and promote the framework of our current belief systems. All that we have known is now offering a different perspective. Be open to expand your mind to offer new perspectives and alternative thinking. For example: I was always told our job as a parent, was to raise our kids and to teach them how to become responsible and well-adjusted adults. Yet it is the process of being a parent that is the framework of learning for all parents.

Our journey of being parents is the lesson. It is in each of our children that yield the lessons we were meant to learn. Wow! What a concept! Going to school, we are told when and where to attend, how we are to learn, to not be late, wait in a line, be courteous to those around us. Be quiet, put up your hand to speak and to always stay within the thought box. Yet in business, we are told to think outside of the box. To not be afraid, to think in unconventional thought patterns and to be competitive at all ventures and to not wait your turn. This in itself, allows us to alter our thinking and to accept the shifting paradigm that is currently crumbling with our evolving society and changing mindset. The old paradigm has been shattered. That being said, here are a few more questions I am asked repeatedly by inquiring minds:

Many people have asked how do you become awakened?

For most, it is in itself a process of growth from tragedy, trauma, expansion and knowledge in which one would immerse themselves in the awakening process, by their thirst for more.

You become enlightened to what the true meaning of life is, accept what you cannot change and become overwhelming calm when faced with adversity and uncertainty. The knowledge that the universe ideally has your back, and ultimately knows what you need.

What's the difference of being awakened and re-awakened?

I firmly believe that we are born, completely awakened, ready to love, ready to give, ready to share. As children we are happy and lovable beings roaming thru life enjoying all of its simplest joys. However, it is in our lives that we are taught to hate, we are taught to be jealous, to be vengeful, and taught to discriminate. It is in this learning that needs to be un-learned in order to completely become Reawakened. Becoming Reawakened is knowing that you have been here before. That knowing feeling that radiates from the very pit of your being. You know that you are changing and that there is so much more to become, to learn and to truly expand.

So, when I say we each must go thru our own path to become reawakened, although the path is similar it varies for each and every one of us. We each must find our way back to oneness and a return to love that will allow us to unlearn what we have been taught.

Questions:

What is a reoccurring issue in your life?

What do you want your purpose in this life to be?

List some hurtful issues that have been hanging over you for a while, with a one sentence of why they remain.

Era Two

➤—I—◆➤—◗—◆—I—◀

Releasing...................... your pain

Re·lease ing (rĭ-lēs′) *tr.v.* re·leased, re·leas·ing, re·leas·es

1. To set free from confinement or bondage:
2. To set free from physical restraint or binding; let go:
3. To cause or allow to move away or spread from a source or place of confinement:

Releasing your pain

*N*ow one may ask… why do we need to release our pain? What does it really do other than make us relive this anguish and hurt? Can we not simply accept it and move forward?

Well yes, but if we are to lose the lesson, then was the pain worth it? When we ask to release the pain of the past relationships and hurts, it is to make room for acceptance, forgiveness and ultimately understanding for what that pain or relationship has brought you. Most painful memories, occurrences and issues in our lives tend to plague us and make us build a wall around ourselves so that we don't experience the hurt again. But is that wise? It has been taught to us to be a natural reflex but ideally, we are taught to shield ourselves from pain. We can very easily remain in the victim stage and now want to release the anger but it is vital. You can not release sooner than you need nor can you be told by anyone. It is a personal journey. As children we regroup faster wanting to try and enjoy life without harboring a sense of fear. So why in adulthood do we hold on to this so tightly? It becomes our comfort zone to remain here and fester and build walls brick by brick. Yet we were all very different as children. Ever see a child who is learning to stand, walk or run? Wanting to play and not being able to keep up? They rebound fast and continue to push themselves until they master what it is that they crave. We must push ourselves to truly review, accept and learn from the mistakes, hurts and issues in our lives. Now you see me write hurts and/or issues but this could be a relationship, a particular person or event that has happened in your life. Remember our stories may differ but the reaction to this hurt affects us all in relatively the same way. For relationship it is key to remember that each is important in your life and regardless of the ending and pain it caused it was meant to happen to bring an acceptance to your life and a lesson that is imperative for you. This is the most important and for most the hardest part of the end of any relationship or issue. In my mentors Gabby Bernstein's book "Spirit Junkie" I finally realised that each of the painful lessons given to me were actually gifts of learning. If we are to accept and review each of our relationships as an assignment, then we are able to review openly and retrieve a better understanding of what that relationship meant and how and why the pain caused us to act and why. This understanding is imperative in order for us to not only move forward to be evolve past the issues that held us back. When we release the pain, we are able to expand our thought process to look outside of our usual self-directed opinion and look at the situation and relationship from another vantage point thus enlightening us to a different view and possibly and varied acceptance.

If you have felt the following:

1. Disappointed in your choices, past and present
2. Anxious about what is not currently working in your life
3. Angry with certain people and how they behave
4. Discouraged by past failures and known setbacks
5. Frustrated by limited opportunities
6. Limited by obstacles
7. Ashamed of yourself

Each and every one of these reasons, just proves you're human in every way.

We each feel these emotions at different times but must understand that each condition's us to remain in the victim mode that feels so comfortable at the time. All growth is uncomfortable, it has to be in order for change to organically happen within each of us. As the noted phrase, amazing things happen at the end of your comfort zone. No one benefits by remaining in victim mode. The key element in comfort is non-movement, no change, no learning or acceptance. It is the stage of being still without progress. The longer we reside in this stage, we tend to build and nurture resentment, build emotional walls around ourselves and become angry and negative in our views. This is highly visible in those who tend to always react in a negative fashion and do not offer a positive or supportive fashion. It is part of our human existence that we are to continue to grow mentally and spiritually to become awakened to these pains and allow the lesson to be learned and adapt past to navigate a more positive outlook.

However, if we are to reawaken to our spiritual consciousness than we must realize that we must not be controlled, nor limited by any of these listed reasons then we can expand and grow extensively. Ideally, we need to identify each of them, acknowledge them and finally release them. By identifying them is to accept that you have volunteered to submit to this thought process. You allowed this feeling to be accepted. By acknowledging them you can correct accept that you have identified to this and can take the necessary steps to change your mindset.

Lastly by identifying and accepting you can therefore release this thought process to move forward from allowing this pain to become part of your baggage for years to come. Release them to the universe as they do no serve you and must be dealt with to lighten your load on this path of self-discovery. These regrets are too heavy to keep carrying though out your life. It is often suggested that journaling or writing down your thoughts for each relationship has affected you is not only therapeutic but a great lease. I also suggest you to review and see if any common thought processes become aware. Some of us are most comfortable of staying in victim mode or have been so hurt in the past that don't allow anyone else in to avoid the hurt.Being able to re-read what you have written down months or years later gives you the chance to review your thought patterns and a time to review if changes are required. This is not only very common but a sign of acceptance and growth. Even if you don't like to write, or journal there are probably thoughts that reside in your mind for years without being assessed or reviewed. As humans, we often hold on to certain thoughts and feelings and play them over and over again in our mind. We then become so stuck on this one particular version of a story that it rarely differs. We then remain in a holding pattern with the same thoughts and feelings that go along with it, that we get stuck in this repetitive cycle.

A repetitive cycle usually becomes so ingrained in our psyche that it can become increasingly difficult to shake from. It really seems that until we grow tired of the repeating story and complaining about the same outcome. We are limited to this repeated cycle. Perhaps by taking time to correctly identify a repetitive story and review from another vantage point would give you a different view and understanding. Allowing you to understand the lesson and allow you to move forward. You have to ask yourself. How long do you want to be replaying this story? What was I supposed to take away from this so I can move forward? When a story or event in your life becomes stuck, it can be very difficult to clear it. This is because the event and/or relationship most likely is stuck due to the thoughts and feelings around it. In order to release and let go of a repetitive cycle or story, we have to approach them differently. We have to identify the repetitive thoughts, review and then change them.

Here are 6 easy steps to helping you release your story.

Step #1:
Take a moment to best identify what story, relationship, occurrence and/or person in your life you are looking to release.

Write on a piece of paper-a) the story, b) the person, and c) elements of pain.

Then read it aloud, allowing your mind to fully understand the full story out loud.

Read it, own it, and get very clear with it, state it and affirm it.

Make sure to write your story down so it is all out on paper.

Step #2:
Take a moment to honor, reflect and respect your story.

If there is any pain, hurt feelings or regret. Own the pain, feel it and allow yourself to truly feel it. If this brings back tears or feelings of hurt, allow yourself to wallow in it for a minute.

Give yourself just a few moments to feel this hurt and allow yourself to say goodbye.

Step #3:
Take a few moments to take a few deep, long and calming breaths.

Release your tears and compose yourself. Then still your mind and then place your hand over your heart. Feel your body for a moment, feel your heart and tune into your heart and allow your natural state be brought back to present.

Step #4:

Once you feel centered again.... You must recite the following, adding in names and things to make it personal if needed. I no longer need this story. I no longer require this story or this pain.

This is my time to re-write my story and own my own victim story. This is my time to release any attachments to this story, for I no longer need it to be defined by. This story will no longer hold me, as this is MY journey. I release.............. The pain, the person, the victim mode, the choices and own the lessons. I will no longer be defined by this pain or this story. I will own this new understanding, the new story and my new lessons. Thank you, thank you, thank you, I am sorry, I love you, and I release you from my heart and from my soul.

Step #5:

Take a moment.

Once you have stated your affirmation and truly felt it, you can consider writing a new story.

This new story should be set in the present and you should be the star of the story if you so choose. You can me absent from the story and just keep the lessons but keep the story focused on you.

Step #6:

At this point it is time to burn your story, to truly release them into the universe.

Rip up all of the papers till they are literally ribbons of papers. Place them in a safe small area such as an ashtray, metal bowl etc.... Light them with a lighter or match, making sure that this is a safe environment. Ensure all of the papers have been complete burned and remain in peace at this moment and in a state of forgiveness, peace and acceptance. Please remember this 6-step process is a merely guide. Please ensure that this must feel good for you and must truly be organic to you as a person. Remember that in order to release, you first need accept, to be open to change and then redirect your energy elsewhere. These stories no longer define you. This pain no longer resides in your heart nor directs your moods, actions nor thoughts. Allow the comfort zone of being in pain to reside and allow yourself to walk forward in a state of release. Crave it, want it, and live in it. When dealing with any sort of pain to reviewing past pains, and anger, it is highly imperative that you ensure to always be cognizant of how this pain affects your body. To be able to release your pain, you must be able to accept it. In doing so, you must also know how this affects your thoughts and manifests within your body and mind.

For some, this means dealing with sadness, anguish, depression, despair, anxiety and anger.

For all feelings, I highly suggest that you seek professional help. Call your family doctor, explain what you have been feeling and ask for a suggested therapist.

For those looking for natural options to only assist in the mental and physical discomfort, I must ask that you look into EFT. What is EFT you ask?

Read along my friend……….. its time you had a friend along the journey in this rabbit hole!

What is EFT?

To be honest, I wasn't too familiar to this treatment, until a few years ago when, I was recently introduced to it during a spiritual Master Class. However, in saying that I had actually preformed and succeeded in preforming EFT on myself by tapping during emotional outbursts and times of stress and anxiety unbeknownst to me for years prior. Almost like an innate auto-response I guess but I still to this very day tend to use EFT without a thought, my body and mind automatically go into action to calm my nerves and self – regulate the anxiety. Its difficult sometimes to wrap your head around why we do things... But I have come to realise that we all do things that is organically natural for us. Hard to understand how a type of treatment can be so innate that our own bodies know what we need without formal training. I mean I know it helped but never knew the reason nor benefits, it only felt right and automatically gravitated to its soothing nature. Similar to a young mother naturally knowing what her body needs during childbirth, the bodies natural ability to heal and sustain itself is unparalleled. It is both amazing and vital to our growth and understanding. The formal definition itself of EFT is Emotional Freedom Techniques. To many this is still a relatively strange term. However, it has become a fairly new fast-evolving treatment within the Energy field of Psychology and treatments. Gaining rapid momentum within the health and wellness communities for its non-medication direction and purely natural approach. This has captured the attention of vast amounts of healers, natural practitioners, scientists, and spiritualists around the world. This non-invasive treatment works on the philosophy and principals of making change to the energy flow within the body itself. For those who prefer the natural approach to healthcare and stress relief, this can offer a new-age, prescription-free relief. This treatment would involve the use of the fingertips to tap on the end points of energy meridians that are positioned just beneath the surface of the skin all over the body. These meridians offer a structured system of energy canals that encompass the whole body. The technique and/or science of this treatment works by releasing blockages within the energy system which are the source of all emotional intensity and discomfort thru out the body. These obstacles within our energy system, challenging us emotionally, limiting our belief systems and affecting our daily behaviours and an inability to live life harmoniously. Much scientific proof has supported, that emotional disharmony is a crucial factor in physical symptoms and disease within the body. This can lead to the manifestation of other issues and symptoms that will prove harmful for the overall health of the human body and mind. Historically, back in the 1920's Albert Einstein confirmed that that everything (including our bodies) was composed of energy. Based on these principles, EFT has the base of modern science work on the base principle that our energy flow is imperative to the human body to function. In the late 1990's, Gary Craig had brought EFT and training of its techniques to thousands of people providing relief for those looking for an non-invasive, non-prescription treatments. Over the last couple of decades, EFT has collected much success and recognition not only from a vast variety of healing professionals, the scientists and spiritualist communities but from a growing number of medical communities. This It is at the heart of the rejoining of the old and new paradigms and embraces a new thought-process of healing as a whole. EFT not only re-establishes the awareness and trust in the natural healing abilities of our mind and body, but also offers prospects to achieving both physical and emotional well-being in a non-invasive treatment that can be offered to all. Please remember, these techniques do not discredit any medical and/or psychotherapeutic professions. At all times one must seek professional advice to best combat their ailments and illness however EFT can always offer a non-invasive treatment as an alternate for much stress release.

How does EFT work?

Our bodies work on the principals of negative and positive energies though out the body. Varying emotions will then cause changes within these energy channels both on a micro and macro level. In the example of a negative emotion this causes a stressful reaction that causing a disruption within the body's energetic system. EFT would work to best assist in clearing up disruptions and eliminating the resulting emotional body stress responses to restore harmony within the body and give relief from any physical and emotional discomfort.

While focusing on the issue you can use your fingertips to gently tap 5 to 8 times each on the 9 of the body's meridian points. Continue to tap as you concentrate on accepting and resolving the negative emotion and recite mantras that will assist in restoring your positive energy's balance.

How do you ask?

By focusing on the specific problem, you can tap your fingers on the end points of energy meridians. This an amalgamation of sending kinetic energy to our energy system, and uncovering and focusing on root causes, facilitates an alignment of the energetic system thereby eliminating the body's response to negative emotion. These acupoints send signals directly to the stress centers of the mid-brain that accesses stress on both the physical and emotional levels. These signals have direct access to the amygdala part of your brain that initiates the body's negative reaction to fear and triggers the fight or flight response systems. This is much like a personal alarm system that when experiencing trauma, and/or fear, the brain is triggered and the body produces cortisol. This stress hormone has an intricate chain reaction response which directly influences the body during any illness, emotional trauma and injury.

EFT tapping points

Tapping points are found thru-out the body along meridian points. These are mapped throughout the body and circulates energy through your body along a specific network of channels. This technique works thru tapping into this energy at any point along this system.

All negative emotions can be felt through a disruption of the body's energy. To be able to offer relief or to restore balance the body you must release the disruption within the energy channels or meridians by tapping certain parts of the face and body. Tapping on these meridian points is quite simple and painless. It can be learned by anyone and can be applied quite easily.

Benefits of this type of therapy

Non-invasive treatment
A positive, and hands-on experience
Little recovery time (based on the individual)
Has long lasting relief from symptoms
Can be self applied
No drugs or equipment needed

Here is a quick rundown of how to preform EFT sequence.

1) Identify the problem you want to focus on. It can be general issue or it can be a specific situation, person or issue which causes you anxiety. When you consider the problem rate the intensity of your anxiety from zero to ten, with ten being the highest.

2) Compose your statement and intention. Setting up your statement should recognize the problem you are identifying and following this statement with an

unconditional affirmation of yourself as a person. Here is an example:

"Even though I feel_____, I deeply and completely accept myself."

"Even though I'm anxious about my i_____, I deeply and completely accept myself."

"Even though I'm feeling this anxiety about my_____, I deeply and completely accept myself."

"Even though I panic when I think about _____, I deeply and completely accept myself."

"Even though I'm worried about how to approach my _____I deeply and completely accept myself."

"Even though I'm having trouble breathing, I deeply and completely accept myself."

Then you can start tapping in the following sequence:
*Note your pressure should be light and consistent of that of when you tap on a table to make a strong yet tolerable drumming sound using the soft pads of your fingers.

1. Start by tapping on the karate chop point on the outer side of your hand. You can use the tips of all four fingers of my right hand to tap the outside of my left hand. Now Tapping 7 in total.

2. Move to the top of the head and then we'll work down the body, making the points easy to remember. Using the fingertips on one or both hands to tap the top of the head. Tapping 7 in total.

3. Eyebrow points are located at the beginning of the eyebrow, nearest the center of the face. Use your index and middle fingers together, on both hands, to tap the two eyebrow points. Tapping again 7 in total.

4. Side of the eye points are located on the bone at the side of the eye. Do not poke yourself! Using the index and middle fingers together, tap on both side of the eye points at the same time. Tapping 7 in total.
5. Under the eye points are on the bone located under the eye about even with the pupils. Using the fingertips of the index and middle fingers, gently tap this spot under both eyes. Tapping 7 times.
6. Under the nose with the index and middle finger of one hand. The spot is roughly midway between the bottom of the nose and the top of the lip. Tapping 7 times.
7. The Chin point is mid-way between the bottom of the lower lip and the chin, in that indentation area. Tapping 7 times.
8. The collarbone spots are located about one inch down and over towards the outside of your clavicle bone. Use four fingers together on each hand to tap the collarbone spots. Tapping 7 times. Some have used the method to tap both at the same time as an alternative.
9. The under the arm point is located about 4 inches below the armpit and to the side of your back. Lifting you left arm, use the four fingers of my right hand to tap under your left arm. Tapping 7 times.

As you tap on each point, make sure to repeat a simple reminder phrase, such as "my anxiety" or "my interview" or "my situation." Now take another deep breath, and once completed the sequence, focus on your problem again to see how intense is the anxiety. Rate it in comparison to a few minutes ago, and give it a rating on the same number scale. This should be lower and this sequence can be repeated several times taking long breaths to allow your body to release stress each time. Repeat as many times as needed. For more information I would suggest to look up more information on EFT and/or an EFT therapist to assist.

Question:

What painful relationship have you been carrying around with you?

Write down three painful relationships that brought you heartache.

Now list how these painful relationships and/or issues that have held you back.

List three

1.

2.

3.

List 3 things goals that you be able to achieve if this pain was no longer affecting you.

Era Three

Rewriting your story

Re·a·ligning (rē′ə-līn′) *tr.v.* re·a·ligned, re·a·lign·ing, re·a·ligns

1. To put back into proper order or alignment:
2. To cause to form new arrangements or to have a new orientation; reorganize:

Rewriting your story

Often easier said than done, being able to set free the hurt, and painful stories that bind us. Being able to set yourself free from your stories is one of the best and most effective way to move forward from past hurts. An effective mindfulness practice for working with self-stories, is to review your story and assess from a different perspective. In holding onto our past hurtful stories this holds us victims to vicious cycle of self-doubts and self-judgments that separates you from others and prevents you from feeling whole and complete. Although no one feels good to be stuck in a place of self-doubt, it's far more arbitrary and malleable than you may think. Practicing mindfulness and self-compassion allows you to see and acknowledge the tenderness and pain in your story without falling under the delusion that the story itself describes and defines who you truly are. Remember it may be your story, a story, but you are not defined by it. The root is to remember that there are lessons within each situation, each painful memory, story, situation and relationship. These are all meant for us to learn from and allow the lesson to be applied to new situations that will allow for growth.

Here are a few key functions to rewriting your story:

Becoming aware-

This may sound simple, but the act of becoming aware of your thought process and how the situation and/or issue has had a sense of control over your life is the first step. It is easy to think that carrying this baggage is easier but by living in a state of awareness, this gives a sense of freedom often as the acknowledgement of any other painful memory, disease, and/or illness and relationships. Becoming fully aware means permitting the truth to set you free. Take the time to grab a note book and write down how your feeling. What are your likes, dislikes or how certain situations make you feel? It is imperative to write down how you feel in order to truthfully become aware of how you are feeling. Remember the truth is in the words of awareness.

Allow the truth in your thoughts-

Allowing truth in your thoughts will permit you to gently soften your reactions to whatever comes up for you in the space of mindful awareness. Allowing the truth is a kind and curious attitude that enables you to look more intensely into your stories and learn from them rather than becoming entranced by them or trying to block them, both of which will just leave you more trapped. By allowing your experience in this way, you can learn to accept all thoughts as opportunities for insight, rather than as proof of anything, including any inherent unworthiness or inadequacy. Thus, allowing enables you to recognize that a thought is a state of being. Our thoughts become us. If dwell on negative after thoughts we will still remain a negative circle of pain. When we allow the truth in, then in that truth we are set free in this thought process.

Witness the narrative-

By witnessing the narrative, is to thoroughly own your story. I don't mean just to say you own your story but to completely believe it and own all aspects of your story. It is imperative to work thru the nuances and thoroughly understand and own your part in your story. Regardless, if you have any regrets on how you acted, what others have done to you, or how painful the story was. By truly owning your story, you can observe the linear narrative from the perspective of a mindful consciousness. Observing this, allows us to review in a nonjudging position in more of a curious manner of thought. Coming from this position, it doesn't allow you to cling to, or avoid anything, nor bare judgement on any parties. With this vital tool, you can look more intensely, into even very painful events with your heart wide open. Then discover what stories do you want to carry with you. Is this your best story? The story is your choice? Remember this is your chance to let go... so, choose well!

Acknowledge the experience-

By acknowledging the actual experience, this allows us to recall accurately, and thoroughly. This practice in reliving and recalling all physical, mental and emotional thoughts, and emotions you experienced, is an important part of this process. We can always best use unassuming phrases to acknowledge your experience, but living thru them with a level of acceptance of the experience itself in a positive manner is vital. Any old tiresome or negative thoughts which you created in the past that held your negative self-talk should be retired. If you can still recall a theme of anger or resentment then you may need to start again. This part of the process is to accept the action, the actual experience, acknowledge the lessons, and own that you lived thru this experience and can speak to the new narrative. Acknowledge all that you notice and be sure to allow the lessons to always take the lead.

Releasing old stories -

Releasing old stories is not for the faint of heart. Learning to release your old stories is to first recognize yourself as separate, from the story itself. This will allow you to not identify from your accustomed thought patterns. It is time now to move past that negative perspective to invite a varied and more positive train of thought. All past visions of past recognition, shame, loss, gain, and pain are all fleeting experiences, not direct characteristics of you. Remember, being in the state of self-projected misery, is not beneficial to anyone. Why not let go? Letting go of all old stories is not only a vital step, but it is the most empowering. Allow the stories to diminish by taking what was most important – the lesson and move past to allow growth internally.

Erase the hate-

By this final process has got to be the hardest and most imperative to the whole process. Without erasing the hate, you will remain in a state of anger and frustration in a perpetual circle of un-happiness. It is always ideal, to ensure that all of the feelings of inadequacy and unworthiness, is eliminated. This, would involve looking at what you're doing, and reviewing the internal dialogue that calls forth comparisons to others and judgments about yourself. When caught up in a negative thought process this will never be beneficial. Releasing the hate, allows you to review the others in the story to be human and to look deeper than the action themselves. Eliminate the state of judgement to allow the hate to dissipate and allow the forgiveness to sweep this hate away. Remember by erasing the hate you can catch up on all that you have missed out on by reclaiming all irreplaceable moment of your life with love! Once all of your stories have been claimed and your lessons have their firm place in your memories, it is time to get intentional. What do I mean? Its time to really get some intention by setting intentions!

Setting intentions-

F or most, setting intentions is an everyday ritual that affects all aspects of life. It can be incorporated in your daily life by simply taking the time, to forward plan your goals. For others, it is as foreign as another language, which is difficult to understand, and seems to interrupt your daily process and is hard to relate to Setting intentions is as easy as outlining what you need and want in your life and sending positive messages surrounding this thought pattern. Setting intensions is simply acknowledging, how you want to feel and letting that feeling direct your choices as it connects your thoughts and actions to an overall goal and purpose. It also allows you to let go of things that are in your life that do not serve you. Although there are many things in life you may want or crave, it is thru our intentions, which will align our thinking processes to allow our mind to the steps to achieving them, and truly enjoying it once achieved. We, as humans tend to always target certain goals and/or achievements and then hope that the feeling of achieving will be amazing. Intention can be explained as the inception of a goal or dream. How powerful is that? Imagine this creative power, which not only fuels us into action, but also realizes and cultivates our needs, from money, love, relationships, and spiritual aspirations to all facets of our lives. Your intention is a direct impulse of consciousness that contains the fuel that which you aim to create and grow.

Remember every single thing that happens in the universe begins with intention. Intentions cannot grow if you hold onto them, as it is only when you release them to the inner most parts of your consciousness that they can grow, flourish and come to fruition. The known classic Vedic text declares, "You are what your deepest desire is. As your desire is, so is your intention. As your intention is, so is your will. As your will is, so is your deed. As your deed is, so is your destiny." So with all of these positive affirmations how do you actually set an intention? Read on............ and prepare your list!

How to set your Intention. Best is to list out your goals:
What are your goals?
What are your dreams?
What do I need?
What can I not live without?

Take the time to really think about it, get emotional, get intentional.

Write it down, keep it near. Once you can clearly visualize your intentions, write it or /them down. Write it on a stickie note and post it on a mirror. It is imperative to ensure that when you set your intention you are clear and concise and keep keyed into this main stream of thought process. Keep it close, keep it clear and keep it on task. This should be made you're your sacred practice. As some may like to light some candles, perhaps play some music and get comfortable and in your Zen moment. Make sure what you write is affirmative and empowering to you specifically. This is about you. When we write our intentions down, we make them real, we give them power.

Here is my 6-step process to intention setting:

Push the Pause Button-

We are all busy, but we can each take the time to pause and engage in our own quiet thought process amongst the noisy chaos of our internal dialogue and conflict. It is during this time that we can shut down the noise, the internal voice to truly allow certain thought patterns to form and grow organically. Most can achieve these thru different forms of meditation, but is not limited to this. Meditations can take you beyond your normal thought patterns and can bring you into a state of silence, stillness and pure consciousness. This to most is the ideal state, to set your seeds of intention. Take this as a time to pause, so your mind can accurately develop a particular thought pattern without ego-driven results, without internal chatter, thoughts of guilt, or any resentments and feelings of lack. This would simply allow the mindfulness and stillness to radiate through.

Time to Release-

Establishing a state of restful awareness is key to release your intentions and desires in a completely organic manner. The best time to plant your intentions is during the period after meditation, while your awareness is centered in the quiet field of all possibilities within your mind. After you set an intention, let it go—simply stop thinking about it. Continue this process for a few minutes after your meditation period each day. If you don't meditate this maybe an option for you to start for a short period of time a day. Check out Chapter four for the process and types of Meditations.

Remain Centered-

All intentions are much more commanding when it comes from a place of contentment and commitment, than if it is derived from a sense of lack or need. Ensure to stay centered refusing to be influenced by any interruptions, other people's doubts and/or criticisms and other related thoughts. Your higher self always knows that everything is all right and will be all right, even without knowing the timing or the details of what will happen. It imperative to always remain centered thorough the day and keep a quiet sense of zen when handling any issues and when trying to navigate thru any past trauma's.

Detach and Surrender-

How does one detach? Well detaching from an outcome is to relinquish your attachments and control of, to a very detailed result and live in the wisdom of uncertainty. This is problematic for most, but we must remember that most attachment is firmly based on fear and/or insecurity. While those who allow the detachment and the unquestioning belief in the power of your true self emerge to the fore front. It is from the intention of faith, and that our lives will work out as it should, that being able to let go and allow all prospects and openings to come your way as they should organically be given, not controlled by us individually. Have faith that and surrender that the universe is all knowing. Detach, surrender, surrender and surrender some more.. when in doubt....surrender some more.

Trust in the Universe-

I get this question a lot. How do you trust in the universe? Well as easy as it sounds... let go of all control. This for myself, being a single mother was one of the most difficult issues of all. To trust in something other than myself and the control that I had on all situations was huge. By allowing your faith in the universe to lessen your focus of control and let our attentive intentions set the countless organizing power of the universe in motion is such a liberating facet of our process. Trust that the divine and infinite power will orchestrate the complete fulfillment of your desires. Do not allow the usual voice of internal reason and control, give air to the usual obsessive vigilance that will push that, the only way to get anything done is to push it thru.

Remember, you have released your intentions. Surrender your intentions to the universe. Once you've written them down and shared them, let them go. Check-in with your intentions frequently, but trust that the universe has got your back.

Check in-

Always remember to check in. Remind yourself daily, of what your intentions are. Be sure to be clear and concise as to

what you want in your life. Being able to develop a spiritual routine or ritual for yourself will only promote more clarity and keep you on task for fantastic outcomes. Remember to commit to a particular time of the day and you may also use this to start in a place of gratitude and align with your intentions.

Things to Keep in Mind When Setting Intentions:

Always be authentic-
What is important to you? Know who you are and what do you really want. What's your mission? What can you offer the world? Who are your heroes? What's important to you? By knowing yourself and being unapologetically authentic. Both personal and professional life will all fall in place. Be authentic and be yourself.

Staying balanced-
Staying balanced and aligned in all aspects of life can be not only beneficial to all, but vital to keeping on track. When trying to balance your life we tend to compartmentalize our responsibilities, and then carefully stack them according to importance. Most of us juggle them dependent on what is happening and what is most important at that time. Remember to always keep from juggling, this is the only way to truly experience balance within.

Always be clear and concise-
Forget the semantics... Be clear, be direct and be concise with exactly what you want. I know many people who will say, "I want more abundance."
Ideally, this is great but this is so vague, because abundance can mean so many things, from family to money to relationships.

Be direct. Place deadlines on your goals and most of all have fun in the experience.

Watch your words-

Have you ever said something and then realized that, what you said was not what you meant? What words did you say? What did you really mean? Did you know the word "want," really truly means "lack?" So saying "I want a new job" comes a place of lack. Choose rather to say "I choose to have a new job." Stay away from the word should as this promotes question. subjective. The term "I hope," leaves the door open for some potential defeat.

Choose to take command with "I will" And / or "I choose". Be precise!

Write, repeat, repeat and repeat-

Write down your intention, say it, repeat it, and repeat again and again. According to many it takes approximately 15 to 20 seconds to set that intention. It has said that idea comes together and a specific energy is formed in this thought pattern. So, in order to give some momentum to your goal make sure to daily…write, repeat, repeat and repeat again!

Always look ahead-

Don't live in the past! Trust me this does not work! Always looking ahead and focusing on what your life will look like when the goal is achieved is essential to being in a state of positivity. This thought process will assist you to create this feeling in your life. Thus, creating a vision board either mentally or physically is vital for success. Always look ahead and plan for your dream to come true.

Always be in a state of gratitude-

Oh me oh my, if I could have learned this lesson years ago. I would have lived a much happier and more tranquil life. Gratitude can bring so many benefits to all aspects of life. We know that even on the most, worst day will always have something we can be happy and grateful for. By writing them down each day can remind us to live in a place of gratitude. This is living a place of bliss! Gratitude is one of the finest ways to create the abundance consciousness, as this will focus on the source of all those things that came into your life. In this process you will be also removing the ego from your daily thoughts.

Always be determined-

Determination is one of the best attributes one could use. Be determined, every moment of every day. Try to never regress. Always remember those who are continually pressing ahead are genuinely successful.

Remember to share-

By being open to share your intentions with the world means this will open you up to being confident. You must be willing to open yourself up to freely manifesting your dreams. When we feel supported, we feel empowered, we feel confident and can be more successful. Remember you never know who can help you manifest your dreams. There is always strength in numbers. Keeping your intentions clear and concise is always key. Remembering them and keeping them near is imperative. How can you keep your mind on task? Well most wear Mala beads that they recite their intensions with and wear throughout the day to keep their motivation clear and remain on task. First though you must understand the beads..... the mala beads that is…

Understanding the beads-

It is widely known that during any time of reflection, to set your intentions that the best utilize the use of Mala beads. I personally thought this to be very similar to that of the Catholic rosary but to each his own. I adapted this practice and can be best utilized in your daily routine as you see fit regardless of your religion or cultural beliefs. In the end you must do what feels right for you. To most Mala beads signify the belief of spirituality, religion or to some a modern type of accessories. Mala beads are mostly used to keep count while reciting, chanting or mentally repeating mantras and intensions. These beads are named after a small town in Thrissur district of Kerala in south India where there is a small Jewish synagogue at Mala Town. They are actual meditation and reciting tools that have been used for thousands and thousands of years. They encourage us to pause, breathe and realign with our deepest intentions, and have been growing in popularity with the current arise of western awareness. Similar to the Catholic rosary beads they remind of us our direction in prayer and motivate us to invest in moments of self-care and compassion. I have often heard of them to be referred to as our "spiritual reminders". While some people may not feel comfortable in using mala beads to set intentions, it is a powerful way to manifest your dreams and achieve your goals. How do you use them?

Hold your Mala beads in your right hand, draping them between your middle and index fingers. Then starting at the guru bead, use your thumb to count each smaller bead by pulling it towards you as you recite your mantra or intention. Most Beads have 108 beads as this needs to be recited 108 times as you travel around the Mala similar to the Catholic rosary beads.

Why 108 beads you ask? Great question...In the ancient Vedic culture, mathematicians recognised early that 108 was the number of all existence. In the yogic tradition, there are 108 Upanishads or often referred to as sacred texts. 108 sacred sites throughout India, and 108 marma points, which are the sacred sites of the body. There were 108 gopis dancing with Krishna in Vrindavan. This number is so deeply entrenched in the Indian consciousness that 108 is the telephone number for emergencies, much like our 911 in the North America. In the Jewish tradition, 108 is a multiple of 18, which is also the number connected to the Hebrew word chai, meaning "life, or alive." As well as in Islam, the number 108 refers to God. There are 108 lines of energy that converge to form the heart chakra. The Sun's diameter is 108 times that of the diameter of the Earth, while the Sun to Earth distance is 108 times the Sun's diameter. So, in all 108 is the number for all existence. By wearing your mala beads during your intention setting process, or during your daily activities will serve as a reminder for your intention.

Allow your intentions, your goals and your dreams to all be encompassed in this daily ritual that this will give you clarity during your day. Especially if you are feeling overwhelmed and/or anxious, always make sure to take or hold your beads/stones and feel the energy of the healing beads and crystals guiding you to your peaceful place. For most, praying with Mala beads or even setting intentions can be a bit overwhelming... but I can confidently say that journaling is an easy option for anyone! Are you game? Read on....

The Art of Journaling

$\mathcal{W}$e all have stories. We are all born to be story tellers. Even as children we can become quite clever in our story telling for all to hear. However, most of what we tell, we do not truly identify with. Have you ever wondered why in the middle of a heated discussion someone may say the exact opposite of what they mean? That's usually become they are not truly meaning subconsciously what their saying. Have you ever wondered if you reworked your story how it would change your view point? Imagine if we could change many tragic or traumatic events in our lives which usually dictate a negative thought process or outcome. Please note that we very rarely hear anyone who tells a tragic story with a positive review. If you were to realign your thought process or reword your story how differently would your outcome be? How amazing that we could determine our own narrative? By journaling, this allows us to reside within our true feelings and inner truth and to expand our thought process to eliminate judgement.

Taking the time each and every day to ponder your thoughts, write them down and allow your mind to release anything this has held your attention, your mind or your thoughts is a great release, especially when some negative things occur. Writing/journaling has also been proven to expand our own thought process, inner dialogue and expand our growth. As most athletes understand that quality equipment helps them perform at their peak. Journaling, by writing down our experiences with God, the divine or the universe (whatever higher power that works best for you), can serve a similar spiritual purpose. Journaling can be viewed as a spiritual cross-trainer that helps as an "aid to all other spiritual disciplines". It becomes a powerful tool the Holy Spirit can use to develop Christ-likeness when we exercise spiritual disciplines such as prayer, Bible reading and fasting. Although most religions do not command us to journal, several of its writers modeled this practice. Many of the Christianity Psalms represent David's journaling, as he struggled with deep spiritual issues. The struggles with the question of evil in his journal, and his agony over Jerusalem's fall. Solomon writes about his search for happiness in his journal Ecclesiastes.

Although the ease of journaling's is not promoted, the profound potential to create spiritual change, it is clearly documented in many wide spread religions. If journaling is new to you or if you've tried it and become discouraged, consider these practical benefits. To this day I still fight with the urge to write but feel that writing down my feelings is somewhat childish as I used to in my childhood diary. In adulthood it is to reveal and release that gives us the most to reflect upon. It will take time to make this part of your daily ritual but after many many months and now years of pushing I can say that this art of journaling has released me to my inner most thoughts and brought a lot of clarity into my life. So pick out some great notebooks grab your favorite, pen, pencil, and markers (no judgement here!) and start writing. NO computers… the art of journaling is that of hand to paper. It is the old release of feeling every word and allowing the feelings to flow. No pick your favorite place to read, grab a cup of coffee, tea or beverage and start writing.

Here are some benefits of Journaling:

Journaling softens our hearts-
Every farmer knows he must work hard till the soil soften, before he plants the seed. In the same manner we often need

our hearts to be softened. By writing out our true feelings we can address what was truly the lesson.

Understand the context-

Life is often happening so quickly around us that taking the time to journal allows us the much-needed time to truly understand the context. Time to stop and reflect on where you are in the bigger picture is key. Journaling should help to discern the difference between the forest and the trees.

Journaling sifts our truth-

Sifting thru the many mixed messages, words and intentions is difficult to navigate easily. Sometimes we unintentionally mix different intentions to our own self-talk, and opinion that would shade our opinion. When we journal and put these thoughts on paper, it's easier to sort out truth from error, very easily.

Clarify your thinking-

Although writing in general helps to disentangle our thoughts, Journaling allows us to be clear and true to our own thinking and what we are feeling. With no one to impress we can be direct and to the point.

Slowing down our pace-

Journaling can act like a administrator to slow our frenzied pace and force us to listen to the Spirit's voice, allowing us to slow down our inner thoughts to put all into perspective. Slow down and allow your feelings to be clearly documented.

Journaling builds our faith-

Regardless of your religion, faiths or belief systems, we remember that journaling builds our faith when we record the many miracles and faithful acts, given to us daily that allow us to be in a place of gratitude, thus building our faith.

Journaling releases our pain-

Journaling usually provides a spiritual release from pressure to release our pain that can prevent future issues. Journaling, can be a spiritual cross-trainer, that offers many spiritual benefits. Use this to release my friends!

Process previous events-

Journaling often helps us to sort through old and new experiences and be very intentional about your interpretation. Use this to work thru old issues if needed!

Note your feelings-

Most feelings are over-rated but being able to notice how your feelings are rated on paper is crucial to self-regulate that perhaps that you may have missed the larger picture. This allows us to regroup our feelings.

Connect with your heart-

Sometimes truly being free to write allows us to connect with our inner most feelings, and allows us monitor how you truly connect with your heart, and your inner voice. By writing down how you truly feel often makes us review how we feel.

Record significant lessons-

Writing things down, not only leads to better retention but also leads to expansive growth on the truly important lessons, that may be easily forgotten if not recorded.

Ask important questions-

Remember journaling is not just about feelings. A journal can be used to ask questions. As well as opens us up to ask what we need to address and ponder. Hence allowing further reflection and growth.

Getting ready:

Get a notebook

Pick out your favorite pen, or pencil

Set a consistent time in a quiet place each day to write

Make a commitment to stick with it

Date each entry

Write from feeling, only do not just record what happened in your life. Write down how your feeling and the experiences that affect your heart and emotions

Periodically review your entries to discover spiritual trends in your life

Highlight whatever pops out of you that merits more review or something you want to address

Now pick up a book and get writing!

Question:

What part of setting intentions do you find difficult?

What can I do daily to ensure I stay on task with my intention?

How can I make this part of my daily practice?

Expand on each allowing words to free flow.

What part of journaling and letting go do I like best?

How can I make this part of my daily practice?

Era Four

Reconnecting with Nature

re·con·nect ing (rē′kə-nĕkt′) *v.* re·con·nect·ed, re·con·nect·ing, re·con·nects
v.tr.

1. To cause to become connected again:
2. To meet or come into contact again after a long absence:

Reconnecting with Nature

*J*f anyone was to have asked me years ago that I would be willingly and truly reconnecting with nature, enough to hug a tree, or to travel to Peru to meditate – stomach down on mother earth, I would have slapped you. You see I enjoyed a clean floor, a polished kitchen and everything in its place. I also did not (and still don't to a certain extent) like getting my hands or fingers dirty! Yep I said it...... I hate dirt under my nails. Now in saying that.... I still love a clean home and don't like dirt in general but I have grown to love nature and build an appreciation of all of the beautiful organic messiness of nature, dirt, grass, and wind that I for years did not want around me. We in our concrete existence tend to familiarize ourselves with a life that is so remotely averse to nature that we become disconnected to the earth around us. We now fail to hear the wind, birds, animals and beauty that surrounds. When we take walks or runs most of us get "plugged in" to music or pod casts that we forget to truly emerge ourselves in nature.

Our highly plugged in world we live in with vacuumed homes, or cars with everything at our disposal. Everything has become so instant, fast food, coffee, 24-hour drive thru or 24/7 stores and delivery. We are highly connected to the vibrant world we live in, yet so detached from one another and nature all at the same time. We have all evolved willing, and slowly to a different version that our modern society has become independent on technology yet disconnect from all that surrounds us. We all live such active and highly technical lives many people live with daily pain and constant stress, anxiety, depression, and fatigue. Many feel off, not centered, aligned, or solid. Most often the case that doctors often can't find the cause and resort to prescribing varying medications that produce side effects like fatigue, poor mood, and headaches. Researchers don't know the specific causes behind the steep increases in a diversity of illnesses, but most say it is because people are eating more unnatural foods than ever and that the ingredients in these foods could be harmful, others point to increased exposure to environmental pollutants. While certain lifestyles approach such as meditation and yoga can help, there are limitations to their effectiveness for many illnesses. All living things on our planet are connected to the ground's electrical energy, humans, animals, and all living matter. In most developed societies, we rarely go barefoot outside or wear natural leather shoes that allow us to absorb the ground's natural energy. In modern society, most of us have lost our electrical roots.

We are so disconnected and this disconnection may be a seriously overlooked cause of human pain and discomfort and the steady rise of chronic illness worldwide. The truth is, we are all ungrounded, and out of touch with Mother Earth. For decades, people have been wearing mostly plastic soled shoes that act as a barrier to the Earth's energy. These beautiful negative ions that mother earth gives us so freely is so beneficial, yet our shoe-wear insulates us from any electrical contact with the Earth pull. What a horrible thought! This is why going to the beach barefoot feels so overwhelming calming! The feel of sand on your feet, between your toes, the rhythmic sound of the waves crashing, the smell of the natural air. This is what truly connects us. Reconnecting with nature is the path to reconnecting to yourself, your higher self, with your soul. It is not only imperative to all scenes of becoming reawakened but imperative for your well being. Trust me, this process is not for the avid couch potato, as you will need to get up and embrace Mother Earth! Reconnecting-hug a tree, listen to a stream, watch the birds, feeding a squirrel is an acquired taste but for most, but only needs to be sampled a few times before you open up to Mother Natures allure. Now not everyone will travel the world to connect with mother earth but trust me once you start on this path you may just want to! This is the art of grounding.

The Art of Grounding

G rounding is a term used to mean re-center and reconnect with the earth, Mother Earth. The Earth itself is like a massive battery that holds a natural, subtle electric charge. This means re-focusing and/or re-establishing yourself to a state of feeling centered, whole and complete. In essence, it is a way to become re-rooted to your physical self, by reconnecting with the physical world. Being grounded also applies to all people, animals and living organisms. This would include plants, water, and the most-tiniest of living matter. As we are electrically grounded, we maintain our body's electric potential, you will feel, more centered, solid, stronger, well balanced, less stressed, and less tense. The easiest way to best describe grounding is actually a feeling of calmness, peacefulness and being centered. Being grounded means that you are centered and balanced with who you are on a soul level, thus meaning you are completed connected to your truest, most authentic self. When you're truly grounded you make decisions that honor and respect your soul's needs on all levels. This is the true benefit of grounding for all beings. This allowing us to truly work on a higher level. It has been scientifically proven to have many benefits.

Healing Benefits of Grounding

There has been much scientific research over the past couple of decades that specifies that our bodies can be protected and helped, when we are electrically connected to the Earth. It is vital for our existence and our well being but must be more firmly intergraded in our lives.

Here are a few examples of benefits:

Instant stress reduction
Improved circulation
Increased emotional and mental clarity
Improved ease within your mind and body
Enhanced ability to speak your truth immediately
Counteract any negative emotions or thoughts
Heightened feelings of peacefulness and calm
Increased psychic and energetic awareness
Decreased Levels of Inflammation and Pain

Being grounded can help relieve inflammation within the body while, reducing night-time levels of cortisol and resynchronizes cortisol hormone secretion. In some cases, it has been known to assist with chronic back pain, and showed a reduction in inflammation in different areas of the body and joints. When grounded, the cortisol hormone begins to normalize which is vital to regulate the body's system. You see that Cortisol is a vital part of our body's stress response system and helps control blood sugar levels, regulate metabolism and inflammation, and assist with memory formulation. When you are grounded the levels of cortisol after sleeping grounded, showed a normalization which leads to better sleep patterns.

Also, when spending regular intervals being grounded it has been found that our circulation improves, aiding in the delivery of oxygen and nutrients to the tissues in the body, which includes better blood flow though-out the body.

How to Reconnect to the Earth

While the research on grounding is relatively new, the practice is timeless. Past societies, shamans, and tribe elders still today go barefoot or wear leather footwear made from hides that still allow the energy of the Earth to rise up into their bodies. It is the benefits of this negative ions that truly radiate within us that we so desperately need.

Personally, I have traveled the world and will say that the feeling that radiates thru your body when you allow yourself the time to reconnect with mother earth is undeniably the most exhilarating feeling. It is not easy to put into words but more so a feeling that can not be recreated in any other manner. Being able to lie stomach down in the sacred lands of Moray, Peru, or to sit cross legged in mediation in the ruins of Machu Piccchu have forever changed me in ways I can only express as miraculous. I have never felt this radiation of warmth, energy and positivity than in these sacred lands. Now, not everyone is able to go running to Peru, but if you can I certainly would suggest it. Honestly, you can reconnect to mother earth anywhere. If your having a bad day, go for a walk outside, if possible, take your shoes off and find a nice patch of grass and walk around. Allow yourself to de-stress and feel the earth on the soles of your feet. Let go of your stress and thoughts and allow your mind to simply be. Hugging a tree is always recommended. I have personally have not met a tree I didn't like. ☺ Personally, connecting to earth can be done any where. Walking on the beach, walking thru the water as the waves rush in, going for a long walks, or merely sitting in a park and admiring nature around you.

Listen to the birds, the smell of the trees, and the sound of leaves rustling by. This can be done almost every where so get out there and explore!

Here are the 30 ways to get grounded:

Go meditate outside in the morning
Get close to a tree, park and/or a forest
Go for a long walk outside daily
Eat more root vegetables
Take time to sit near stream/river and listen to the rushing water
Take time daily to breathe in fresh air
Surround yourself with natural incenses or candles
Spend one on one quality time with your pets
Do yard work in the bright sun light
Hunt for crystals and get immersed in the beauty of rocks
Get physical with exercise daily
Lay in the sun, get some vitamin D and be sure to breath in
Grow your own herbs and vegetables
Hike to natural rock if possible, a mountain or cliffside
Read a good book outside if possible
Completely disconnect from all technology for an extended period of time
Lay on your back and look at the clouds, allowing your mind to wander
Pamper your physical body with a massage, pedicure, or manicure
Have a real conversation without any technology present
Work on an intricate craft that requires your hands
Go bird watching, see, feed and hear them
Listen or create your own earthy music

Now that we can all say we have truly connected with Mother Earth – "Gaia" as many call her, we can attest that we have hugged a tree and ran barefoot in the earth. Now its time to dig deeper inside ourselves and start with meditation. Now for those who will quickly say this is not for them… please please give it a chance. I also thought this was a practice that would not integrate into my life, my mind and my schedule. Well years later and I often crave to meditate and feel off if I haven't during my regular day. Please read on…..

Meditation

*W*ell it is a practice that takes time to master and truly become a daily ritual. The practice of meditation for myself was a slow and steady process of knowing that it takes time and that with each mediation would bring me closer to truly reaping the benefits. The known benefits to meditation are widespread and the practice has been growing with an increasing rate making Meditation more of a common practice. It has been well documented, that the benefits of meditation in its various forms, support the cure of many ailments. It aids us in so many aspects, of the human condition that it is becoming an aspect of most doctor's tool box regardless of age, gender, religion or culture. However, this thought process and concept of treatment, has not only been repeatedly questioned, but also under much scrutiny by many, due to its various origins along with societies limited outlook past the popular cocktail of medicines available.

It is from the conventional mindset that Western medicines can cure all, however over the last couple of decades, the awareness and benefits of meditation has become increasingly popular and mainstream, especially in the treatment of migraines and managing stress. Meditation as an active daily ritual, could be at the root of many cures as well as for prevention to many common ailments that currently plague our society. Increasingly the power of meditation, for treatment of conditions such as stress, anxiety and depression, which are linked to the main cause of migraines have become more known, used and accepted in our aging society and healthcare systems. A migraine for most is a disorder of continual stress, and a hyper-excitable brain, and is recommended for those sufferers to adopt a stress-reducing lifestyle incorporating habits of regular meals, adequate fluid intake and deep sleep, sensible use of medication, to achieve emotional stability. Migraine headaches are deemed "vascular" headaches, that are due to the enlargement of blood vessels in the brain, that releases chemicals that cause inflammation, pain, and even further enlargement of the blood vessel. Pain from migraines can be intense with throbbing or pounding pain, sometimes accompanied by nausea, vomiting, and extreme sensitivity to light and sound along with some sensory warning symptoms-such as flashes of light, blurred vision and/ or blind spots.

Meditation is an extremely effective treatment for headaches as meditation releases serotonin into the system, which assists in constricting blood vessels within the body and further reduce the inflammation. Medication on the other hand is proved highly effective, however prolonged use of any and most medications only leads to additional medications. The best course of action would be in seeking to lessen the severity, and duration of migraines and more importantly, prevention. Deriving from a long family lineage of migraine sufferers, I had been plagued for years with the ritual of traditional medicines, treatments, doctor's visits and the traditional suggestion to combat stress. If the cause itself can be systematically diminished by meditation in the spiritual healing process, then the solution is to lean toward a preventative action rather than a quick cure of medication. The current art of spiritual healing has not only evolved along with other types of medicine but is now growing in popularity across many demographics and countries and gaining ground in support of functional medicines. To better understand meditation, we must first recognize the concept and process of spiritual healing to fully comprehend the complexities of this practice. Spiritual healing focuses on the mind-body-spirit connection, which is also known as the holistic experience. This practice with spiritual healing can outline multiple benefits for the mind, body and spirit.

Benefits of Meditation on your brain
Improved mood and memory retention
Alleviate mental distractions
Increase brain capacity and clarity
Improved thought process and problem solving

Benefits of Meditation on your body
Enhance immune responses within the body
Alleviate symptoms of stress
Decrease elements of fatigue
Reduce impact of physical and/or emotional pain

Benefits of Meditation on your spirit
Increase the state of flow
Improve empathy and gratitude
Attain true enlightenment

Now that we have outlined all of the benefits of meditation and why we should all enjoy this practice here are the types of meditation. Remember it maybe a great idea to try each and see which one best fits your fancy. Remember it is all personal. Whatever feels right is right for you. There is no wrong choice. You can also change your preference dependant on what your needs are. How wonderful! Read on.............

Now There are many various disciplines of meditation that have also been studied for their positive effect on holistic health. Each method outlines their base of the mind-body-soul connection which is key to our well-being which are each beneficial and all are equally positive for the well being our over-all mental, physical and spiritual health.

Yoga and Meditation

The word "yoga" actually means "union with the divine", how fitting! The stretching exercises of that we in the west associate with yoga were originally designed, thousands of years ago, to help the practitioner gain control of their own life force. This force or spiritual energy known as Kundalini. These stretches, however, are not the only aspect of yoga. Meditation is also a key facet of yoga and work in tandem to align the body and mind.

Zen

Zazen is a type of meditation unique to Zen Buddhism that functions at the heart of the practice, Zen is the Japanese word for meditation. Traditionally called Dhyana in India, Zen meditation is a very simple yet precise method of meditation, where the correct posture is imperative. Zen is a path of awakening: awakening to who we really are, and awakening the aspiration to serve others and take responsibility for all of life.

Transcendental

This meditation comes from the Hindu faith and involves the use of sound and mantras. Transcendental Meditation is a simple, natural and effortless technique practiced 20 minutes twice each day while sitting comfortably with the eyes closed. The TM technique is easy to learn and enjoyable to practice. The TM technique allows your mind to easily settle inward, through quieter levels of thought, until you experience the most silent and peaceful level of your own awareness.

Mindfulness

This Buddhist practice goes beyond Vipassana to build total awareness. Mindfulness meditation is unique in that it is not directed toward getting us to be different from how we already are. There are three basic aspects worked with in this meditation technique: body, breath and thoughts. Instead, it helps us become aware of what is already true moment by moment.

Vipassana

Vipassana is the oldest of the Buddhist meditation practices, that is a gentle technique, and is very thorough, based on the ancient system of training of the mind. This method derives directly from the Satipatthana Sutta a discourse attributed to the Buddha himself. Vipassana is a direct and gradual cultivation of mindfulness and awareness that can be taught and practiced daily.

Regardless of which Meditation practice you chose to practice, or that best aligns with you in your life and schedule, it is a definite benefit regardless of age, race, religion or gender to incorporate a form of daily meditation for overall and long-term health.

Regardless of how long or how frequent the impact of meditation and mindfulness can be severally impactful on your life, your mind and your body. Find the tools to allow this Food for thought-meditation can be done while walking, for long or short periods of time and can be also tracked thru online apps. My suggestion here would be to try different types of mediation, get informed and search the internet, and apps to see what best fits your lifestyle and preference. What can be added to enhance your meditation is crystals. Yep! I said crystals. You know I was going to finally get here.....

The Healing Pull of Crystals

For as long as I can remember, I have been drawn to all types of crystals. They would all differ in shapes, colors, weight and clarity. As a child, I would often wonder, from what far land, had this stone been taken from and the travels involved to find themselves in my little hand. I had a small yellow pouch hat I would stash away and keep them close, and oh did they feel so powerful in my hands. I craved to hold them tight and feel their energies radiate throughout my body. It's like they gave me light, energy and power. It was like they had the power of Superman's kryptonite! It wasn't until many, many years later, that I discovered the healing powers of crystals I had been aware of crystals in my life, as the beauty and power of crystals and other stones have been well documented but not everyone would hold and use them for their healing and / or spiritual power.

Amazing to think that there are literally, thousands of different crystals on this planet of ours, however only a very few are used in crystal healing. Stones and crystals can be used not only in jewelry, in religious artifacts but in history as well. Crystals have been sought after for many purposes, crystals have been best utilized throughout history in all corners of the world, though out all religions and for all genders.

The History of Crystals

For us to truly date crystals would be to date most common stones in the earth it self. As humans we have always had an attraction to both stones and crystals, so for us to comment on their use in history runs hand in hand with historical events. The use of various crystals dates back many centuries to talismans and amulets as well as for healing and protection, and adornment thorough out history. Crystals have held their place and importance in history in many cultures, and events throughout history. These stones date back from the Egyptians, Romans, Native Americans and others that have all had a special connection with crystals, that was held by their belief system and religion. Ancient Egyptians believed crystals to be protective and shielding such as with talismans for protection and healing stones. This can be also stated for countless cultures around the world who all collected them for not only their beauty but for their inherent properties as well. There are many historical suggestions to the use of crystals that come from magic formulas. While others use crystals in their jewelry and adornment. Dependant on location different cultures and religions would attribute qualities that would be of use to them specifically. For example, Jade was highly valued in ancient China and were used in beads, put in armour, musical instruments, and chimes.

Crystals in Religion

Many Crystals and gems have played an important part in all religions, and often mentioned throughout the Bible, in the Koran and many other religious texts. The Kalpa Tree, which represents an offering to the gods in Hinduism, is said to be made entirely of precious stone and a Buddhist text from the 7th century describes a diamond throne situated near the Tree of Knowledge. The ruby was also highly revered, as it represented an inextinguishable flame, and was purported to preserve both the physical and mental health of the wearer.

The treatise lists many other gemstones and their properties. In Europe, from the 11th century through to the Renaissance, a number of medical treatises appeared extolling the virtues of precious and semi-precious stones in the treatment of certain ailments. Stores when used in combination with herbal remedies increased their qualities of strength or protection which was always a concern in many different areas in history. It was also believed that gemstones were corrupted by the original sins of Adam, could possibly be inhabited by demons, or if they were touched or handled by a sinner, their positive virtues would depart. Therefore, they should be cleansed and consecrated before wearing. There is a definite echo of this belief today, in the cleansing and programming of crystals before use in any crystal healing. Different crystals and stones are often said to have different properties and effects and heal the body. Having them around you brings out an energy that neutralizes any negative vibrations and creates harmony within the area they are stored and with those who wear them. Crystals not only help you with attaining positivity, alleviating moods, financial gain, but also have cures for protection from the evil eye.

Crystals are all natural and created from the earth so each crystal has unique healing properties derived from the minerals from which it is composed. These properties can be described as subtle, amplifying, focusing, directing, absorbing, diffusing and transmitting all different levels of healing energy.

New Spiritual Culture

Although crystals have been used in almost everything from electronics to home décor, in symbolic unions such as engagements, marriage and other religious celebrations. It wasn't until the early 1980's that their healing qualities commenced to gained momentum as a genuine healing method and art of healing. Today you can find healing crystals almost everywhere.

With the increase of the practical practice of healing methods drawn from old and ancient traditions and healing modalities, not only authenticated but deepened our quest to see out all crystals for their wide range of abilities. To date there are now thousands of books available on the subject, millions of professionals who best use the benefits of crystal healing.

Crystal therapy now crosses the boundaries of both religious and spiritual beliefs, and is no longer singularly viewed as the domain of alternative culture, but as an acceptable and complimentary therapy, that is offered in colleges all around the globe.

Crystal in Healing

Crystal healing has been used since the dawn of the human race. It is a fact that crystals emit tiny electrical impulses which activate the human body's neurological system in a subtle manner. Different crystals possess their own unique energy signal, producing different effects. In the crystal healing process, you keep the chosen stones on the specific chakras to heal the body and uplift your spirits. Many crystals have been used by laying them in coordination with the body's energy field, energy centers and energy pathways. The body's energy field are also known as the aura, the chakras and the meridians. Having correct placement of crystals on the body will not only promote emotional and mental harmony but will also allow the body to experience the perfect conditions to benefit and heal naturally. Crystal therapy is generally a noninvasive, holistic treatment for both mental and physical ailment. Healers and subscribers to this specific type of treatment often rely on precise placement of crystals on the body meridians in order to heal and relax the body and mind for healing purposes. The ancients didn't have access to the scientific information that we have today, however, people around the world seemed to instinctively be drawn have a deeper understanding of their value and meaning in our everyday life and in the world in general. I did have the pleasure of training with a Reiki Master many years ago, who shared with me the easier ways to understand the healing powers of different crystals and stones is to best identify by the properties of the color.

This also fell along with the colors of the Kundalini chakras along the body. As many Healers, priests and Shamans before us long used crystals for their unique properties it has become known that each crystal's color and properties make each special and unique on how the responded to the varied areas of the body.

Colors of Crystals-

White or most clear stones symbolize the potential to reflect all energies around them. White is related to the concepts of clarity, cleansing and purification and promote healing, manifesting and meditation.

Black stones will show you the hidden potential of any situation. Black is solidifying and manifesting that holds all energies and are usually grounding and protective.

Red crystals (first chakra) are usually found to stimulate, activate and energize and are great to use daily for all physical movement, motivation and protection.

Indigo crystals (seventh chakra) are definitely my favorites and are linked to your "third eye" chakra, which is to strengthen your intuition, perception, and overall understanding.

Violet crystals tap into inspiration, imagination, empathy and the sense of service to others, while assisting to rebalance the extremes within the systems of the body.

Purple or Amethyst (sixth chakra) is usually deemed one of the most useful all-purpose healing crystal, as it is universally applicable in meditation, it can enhance intuition and is also excellent for lucid dreaming.

Green crystals (fourth chakra) are usually associated with the heart, as they attend to balance emotions, encourage personal growth, and bring about a sense of calm.

Blue crystals (fifth chakra) are often associated with the throat chakra and all elements of communication, such as taste, smell, voice and sight and is well known for its ability to promote clear communication, courage and confidence.

Rose colored crystals have a tender way of assertive things towards a resolution. Rose Quartz is possibly the best known of most pink stones, and has a calming and supportive effect, that supports unconditional love, self-love and loving gratitude of others.

Orange crystals (second chakra) combine energizing and focusing qualities, allowing creative and artistic skills to flourish and for increasing motivation, enthusiasm and energy.

Yellow crystals (third chakra) best recount to the bodies effectiveness to deal with any fear, stress and happiness.

The Citrine Quartz Crystal, is often a bright and vibrant yellow that helps keep the mind focused, clear and on task. When discussing Crystals, it is almost impossible to not touch upon the colors and principals of the chakra. What is a chakra you ask? Great question, this will set the stage for some colorful answers.... Read on.

The Chakra's

*N*ow my background didn't really prepare me for the lessons or understand of Chakra's, as this was not something I had ever heard of. However, I was in store for a learning that to this day still allows me to understand the underlying issues I have thorough-out my body.

This belief system and tradition can be traced back to ancient roots originating in India between 1500 and 500 BC, found in the oldest texts called the Vedas which are the oldest collection of writings which was recorded by the upper caste Brahmins who were descendants from the Aryan stock. These writings covered this ancient knowledge referring to a map of the chakra system that allows life energy to flow, allowing the awakening of the body's individual awarenessThe original meaning of the word Chakra as "wheel" denotes to the chariot wheels of the rulers, called cakravartins. Which was also used as the reference to the sun. These texts form the basis of our understand of chakra theory and Kundalini yoga in today's society.

The history of the chakra systems has become a New Age practice it has many interpretations to the meaning and functionality. In the ancient traditions there are seven basic chakras, that all exist within our body. Our modern physiology can note that this ancient practice has aligned the seven main nerve ganglia that emanate from the human spinal column.

Here are the 7 primary chakra colors:
Red – First chakra
Orange – Second chakra
Yellow – Third chakra
Green – Fourth chakra

Blue (sapphire blue or turquoise) – Fifth chakra
Purple (or deep indigo) – Sixth chakra
Indigo or White (sometimes purplish white) – Seventh chakra

While the chakra colors reflect different frequencies of light and energy associated with each energy center, their meaning may be related to the function of its associated chakras and general symbolism.

When you see or use the following colors, you could make the following associations:

First Root Chakra-Red: Red is the color of the root chakra, symbolizes safety, survival, grounding, nourishment from the Earth energy. Note that in chakra healing practices, red may denote inflammation at the physical level.

Second Sacral Chakra-Orange: Orange is the color of the sacral chakra carries meanings associated with emotions, creativity, sexuality, and is associated with water, flow.

Third Solar Plexus Chakra-Yellow: is the color of the solar plexus chakra symbolizes mental activities, intellect, personal power, will.

Fourth Heart Chakra-Green: Green is the color of the heart chakra connected with love, relating, integration, compassion.

Fifth Throat Chakra-Blue: Blue is the color of the throat chakra symbolizes self-expression, expression of truth, creative expression, communication, perfect form and patterns.

Sixth Third eye Chakra-Purple (or deep indigo blue): Purple is the color of the third eye chakra evokes intuition, extrasensory perception, inner wisdom.

Seventh Crown Chakra-White (or Indigo): White is the color of the crown chakra, associated with the universal, connection with spirituality, consciousness.

Now, understanding the chakras reside as an energetic wheel or vortex of energy found in the subtle body is a thought-process that deserves much understanding and training. The Prana, commonly known in the practice of yoga is the life force energy, circulates through various nadis, pathways of energy. These seven main chakras align with the Sushumna Nadi, or central channel. When you understand chakras, we tend to become more in-tune with our body's so rather than fixating on the physical, we are able to access the areas in our body that require help or maintenance. Chakras can influence our lives in the colors that we surround ourselves. Each chakra is associated with a color found on the rainbow. So, we can add a fun, new dimension in which we can better understand ourselves and relate to our surrounding environment. Your body is a well of wisdom and by diving into this ancient system you can better understand yourself and lead a bright life filled with optimal vitality. So think of the color and chakra you are looking to heal and surround yourself in the colors of the rainbow!

Questions:

How do I best feel to re-connect to my inner self?

What types of meditations do I most align with?

Pick a color that you quickly resonate with.

Which color stone and chakra is that?

Era Five

Re-kindling.............. the Love

re·kin·dle ing (rē-kĭn′dl) *tr.v.* re·kin·dled, re·kin·dling, re·kin·dles

1. To relight (a fire).
2. To revive or renew:

Rekindling the love

*A*h............................. Rekindling the Love – love to all humans, to all creatures, oh nature to yourself and to the Divine. This for most is difficult if you find yourself in a time of despair or difficulty. What I have learned that it is in that time that is the most vital and the most valued. Thinking and giving of yourself in a time when we would mostly reside inwards and engage in self pity is such a huge leap. How do you, when you have nothing to give? This was such an imperative lesson for me as I often find myself upset or angry not realizing that this was the best way offset my mood or what was troubling me. Common human behavior is to either push outward and express your despair to many around you, or to reside inwards and process internally and alone. Even though, I don't engage in self pity I often prefer the latter and reside inward to shelter myself from questions. In a world in which is based on give and give some more. It seems odd that we rarely make time to give ourselves some love, and affection.

What does reinvest is love mean? Well as easy as it could be explained, tell the people around you that you love them. Message, Text, Email or PM them each with a simple message of love and the outpour of what you get back will astound you. I don't personally believe that all needs to be posted on Facebook but if you feel so compelled rock it with your own flavor. Reinvesting in love also means to love yourself, to be in honor of yourself. For what you need, what you require. A great book, that so inspired this chapter is from *Gala Darling – Radical Self Love*. A definite must for anyone who is looking to be inspired, to look at loving yourself, and the world thru different eyes, a kick in the backside with her sparkly wand. Gala, I love you and thank you for this "Radical" book. It is once reading this book that I realised that I needed to love more so when in chaos. To love more when I'm upset, to love more when in a difficult situation and above all remember to love of myself to be the best I can be. Mothers all over the world … here me… Take time to Love yourself. Take time to reset yourself in love and appreciation. It could be just some quiet time to read your book, take a bath or to go get a pedicure. Investing in self-love is as important as showing your kids love thru all of the loving things you do for them. It is in the times of despair that were so hard for me. Feeling love when you just got yelled at, at work, or had a fight with your partner, or best friend. I it so imperative to reset this button to default

Self-Love

*W*hat is Self-Love anyways? I have to be honest, as a mother of two I never fully understood nor bought into this term and always felt odd to this concept. Although Self-love is a relatively new and widespread term these days, we have very little information as what this actually means for each of us. Yet it has interjected into mainstream dialogues in a very large way. Most self-help guru's will use the term self-love to best describe how to emotionally, mentally and physically take care of yourself. The term itself has often left many wondering what does that truly mean? It wasn't until I met author "Gala Daling" and read her book Radical Self-love that I truly realized the actual importance of how this new sweeping concept of loving yourself become more apparent in my desire to improve myself. "You only loved yourself, this wouldn't have happened to you." "You can't love another person until you love yourself first." These are just a few of the self-love directives that we give or get to suggest a way to more living fulfillment. Self-love is imperative to al living beings. It is one of the fundamental cores of all of our belief systems and is deeply rooted in most of our internal decisions. It influences who you pick for a mate, the image you project at work, and how you cope with the problems in your life. It is so important to your welfare that I want you to know how to bring more of it into your life.

What is self-love, then? Is it something you can buy in a beauty makeover or a new set of clothing? Can you get more of it by reading something inspirational? Or, can a new relationship make you love yourself more? The answer to all of these questions is No! Although they feel good and are gratifying, you can't grow in self-love through these types of activities. Since, self-love is not simply a state of feeling good. Self-love is a state of appreciation for oneself that *grows from actions* that support our physical, psychological and spiritual growth. Self-love is dynamic; it grows by actions that mature us. When we act in ways that expand self-love in us, we begin to accept much better our weaknesses as well as our strengths, have less need to explain away our short-comings, have compassion for ourselves as human beings struggling to find personal meaning, are more centered in our life purpose and values, and expect living fulfillment through our own efforts.

Steps for Self-Love.

1) Practice good self-care-You will love yourself more, when you take better care of your basic needs. People high in self-love nourish themselves daily through healthy activities, like sound nutrition, exercise, proper sleep, intimacy and healthy social interactions. Take time for yourself and do the things that feed your soul and body. Pedicures are my favorite, but some people

prefer full body massage if this is what assists in healing your body then budget accordingly and go get pampered.

2) Set restrictions-You'll love yourself more when you set limits or say no to work, love, or activities that deplete or harm you physically, emotionally and spiritually, or express poorly who you are. There are restrictions to all that we do. So choose wisely and always remember that you are always in control of your life, yourself and those around you.

3) Shield yourself-Bring in the right people into your life. Remember you are and become those who you hang out with. So please remove those that suck you of energy and wish them well. These are those people (you know who they are!) who take pleasure in your pain and loss rather than in your happiness and success. There isn't enough time in your life to waste on people who want to take away the shine on your face that says, "I genuinely love myself and life". You will love and respect yourself more. So my suggestion is release them and allow yourself the love and appreciation to not engage in the negative outlook of these people.

4) Forgive yourself-We humans can be so hard on ourselves. The downside of taking responsibility for our actions is punishing ourselves too much for mistakes in learning and growing. You have to accept your humanness (the fact that you are not perfect), before you can truly love yourself. Practice being less hard on yourself when you make a mistake. Remember, there are no failures, if you have learned and grown from your mistakes; there are only lessons learned.

5) Live Intentionally-You will accept and love yourself more, whatever is happening in your life, when you live

with purpose and design. Your purpose doesn't have to be crystal clear to you. If your intention is to live a meaningful and healthy life, you will make decisions that support this intention, and feel good about yourself when you succeed in this purpose. You will love yourself more if you see yourself accomplishing what you set out to do. You need to establish your living intentions, to do this. If you choose just one or two of these self-love actions to work on, you will begin to accept and love yourself more. Just imagine how much you'll appreciate you when you exercise these seven-steps to self-love. It is true that you can only love a person as much as you love yourself. If you exercise all of the actions of self-love that I describe here, you will allow and encourage others to express themselves in the same way. The more self-love you have for yourself, the better prepared you are for healthy relating. Even more, you will start to attract people and circumstances to you that support your well-being.

6) Become mindful-People who have more self-love tend to know what they think, feel and want. They are mindful of who they are and act on this knowledge, rather than on what others want for them. Acting on what you need rather than what you want. You love yourself when you can turn away from something that feels good and exciting to what you need to stay strong, centered, and moving forward in your life, instead. By staying focused on what you need, you turn away from automatic behavior patterns that get you into trouble, keep you stuck in the past, and lessen self-love.

Self-love is one of these concepts that you just get. You don't logically understand it, you simply feel it. In my case I read about it, I practiced what was suggested in books and articles, and then one day I just got it. My mindset shifted, and I started to slowly change my thought process and how I treated myself. I started to love myself. Read about it, research it, learn, and discover how it makes you feel. Keep searching, till you feel that you have embraced how you need to love yourself. I will simply click, kind of like learning a dance or the poses in yoga. like You may need to keep realigning yourself and self-talk to practice self-love daily but your practice will allow you to grow. Soon you will simply align to practicing self-love daily.

One of my favorite quotes from "Return to Love" Marianne Williamson is "It takes courage...to endure the sharp pains of self-discovery rather than choose to take the dull pain of unconsciousness that would last the rest of our lives. This quote has stayed with me and I have been able to adapt many traits of self-love that I practice daily but have now been able to also embrace the concept of living a heart-based life. What does it mean to live a heart-based life you ask? Read on... I am so delighted you asked!!

Living a heart-based life

From a very young age, we are often taught to make sense of this vast everchanging world we live in and do our best to navigate and lead our lives in a compassionate and loving way.

Yet, we are trained in schools to think logically, strategically and try our best to compartmentalize everything into a resemblance of order and direction. We go to school to learn, we work to live a good life, but when can we listen to your heart so we can live to our outmost capacity? Our intuition is an innate trait that we all have, that allows us to create a deeper sense of understanding and peace within our life. It is a natural sense and awareness of the world and is a part of who we are yet, we often forget to follow our hearts. When we listen with our hearts, the stress, fears and internal dialogue we create in our minds, lose their power. This is our minds spinning out of control with internal stories, influenced with anxiety, but it is our heart act as our core compass. When we listen with our heart's dialogue, it is easy to decipher what is true in our minds and what is an stress directed narrative that is false. Our inner heart's voice will always show us what is factual, and will always lead us towards seeing and feeling love. This is where deep empathetic understanding stems comes from.

Now I'm not here blazing in on my colorful unicorn, preaching I am the best at this! I am in transition like everyone else on this planet, and work hard each and every day to achieve a heart-based life, but ideally listening and attending to my heart's dialogue has forever transformed my life. Ok, so someone out there has to be asking….. Ok What is my heart's dialogue? As much as we have an internal dialogue that tells us we are not smart enough, tall enough etc.. our hearts dialogue tells us the truth. We all KNOW we are never as bad as we think we are. Our heart is our centre our core and internal compass. It regulates us, when we wind out of control. I've gone from being angry, despondent, and stressed filled, to finding passion in all that I do. Now remember, listening to your heart's dialogue is not easy, as is living a heart-based life is not going to eliminate all of your problems. However, it will give you a flashlight when the lights go out what you need to set your focus on. Allowing your heart to direct your focus on only the important things in life that serve meaning in your life. After years of running thru life stressed, and multi-tasking, living a heart-based life has now become my way of life. I have learned to find the joy in all that I face without taking life too seriously and finding happiness in all aspects of my day and try to laugh at every turn.

Here are a few tips to help in your heart-based journey:

1. Becoming aware of your inner voice

    First thing you need to do is to be aware how you treat yourself and the inner dialogue you use. We all talk to ourselves in our minds, but we are not always fully conscious of that voice. Pay attention to your words. Notice what you tend to tell yourself most often. Self awareness here is key. Take the time to truly hear your voice. Here are a few great exercises to help identify your inner dialogue.

    Start writing these thoughts in a journal to organise your thoughts.

    Keep a journal in your purse

    Highlight the negative comments to track your progress

2. Taking control of your inner voice

    What you hear in your head could have been there your whole life. A running narrative of negative talk that sole purpose is to put yourself down. Take control! You might have not paid attention to it before, but negative talk affects us in so many ways. The truth is, that you've been hearing these messages for years and the more we hear, the more we believe in it. Which means that all those negative things you say to yourself have become your strongly held beliefs.

    But it is time now and you can change them. Step by step.

Similar to tip 1. it is important to track your thoughts.

Write down all inner thoughts

Color code positive and negative with different highlighters

Setting up a reward system for 10+ positive comments such as a treat.

Set up goals for 1 week, 1 month and then 2months monitoring your progress.

3. Find your inner child

To find your inner child you need to imagine yourself as a child. Tuning into that inner child allows you to look at yourself without judgement. To see yourself as this little, vulnerable creature, that simply wants to be loved. Your feelings will be pure and directed by love. Want to truly connect and find your inner child. The moment you envision yourself as a child, you'll notice that the harsh judgement will simply melt away. After all, we all have our inner children within us. There are needs that were never met when we were very young – and we carry these needs into our adult lives. We might suppress them, push them into subconscious and not even realize they are there – but I guarantee you, there are. Treating yourself like a child allows you to cater to those needs.

Here are few exercises for you.

Go to a playground and sit on the slide or swings

Visit your childhood school yard and remember the time spent playing.

Look thru old photos of yourself as a child to reconnect.

Write your adult-self a letter from your child-self remembering all of your aspirations and dreams you wanted and dreamed about.

4. Time to date yourself

This hands down has got to be my ultimate favorite part of the whole process. So how do you date yourself? Well what do you do when you go out on a date? Getting ready, treating yourself to a new outfit or movie is just part of this process. Think of all the things that you enjoy, that bring you pleasure happiness and joy, and simply do them with yourself. It's to befriend yourself and feel completely happy and whole even when there is nobody else next to you. We need to stop depriving ourselves from things that we like and that make us happy. Give yourself permission to do things you enjoy. Spending time doing things just because you like them should be just as important. Here is a few suggestions:

Take yourself out for a nice dinner
Paint (or do any other type of art that you enjoy and that allows you to express creatively)
Write some poetry or lyrics to a song.
Visit museum or historical landmark
Try a new heart healthy recipe
Make your favorite tea and read your favorite book
Binge watch some romantic comedies
Buy yourself a new outfit
Get pampered with a manicure and/ or pedicure
Go to Spa for a healing massage
Take a meditative yoga class
Take a Dance class and allow your body to move
Listen to your favorite music

Play with animals
Go for a long nature walk

5. Listening with your heart
We were all given, 2 eyes to see, 2 ears to hear, 1 mouth to speak, 2 legs to action and support, 2 arms and hands we have been given to help others. So, its amazing to me, that all of us can listen, but many of us listen to respond, and not to actually listen to truly listen. Socrates was quoted as stating" "Nature has given us two ears, two eyes and but one tongue to the end that we should hear and see more than we speak." There is a lot of truth to that, but in our modern society, it is often the loudest who is heard, so being heard becomes the key characteristic we hold onto with importance. However, is that the truest way to live? It has been a proven theory that we listen mostly to respond to each other, offering an opinion and rarely truly listen to what the other person is saying or trying to convey. It's a basic human function, yet proper communication still seems to eludes us.

This lack of attention, can often lead to issues in most relationships, work situations, learning environments, and issues connecting to others. It stands to reason with so many people talking, and so little of us listening, we will often mis-interrupt, mis-understand and mis-communicate with one another. As humans, we pride ourselves with a great comprehension of human interactions, you would have thought we could have mastered this by now. Try to listen to truly listen, try to forget your opinion and listen to hear the other person. Like being in a conversation with the most important person in the world. Listen with an open heart to truly hear them and what they mean, what their saying and what this means to them.

How to connect while listening:
Connect with their eyes. Lock into their gaze and do not look away.

Get in-tune with their body language, and notice changes
Watch your own body language and how you are to be perceived.

Watch your words, and how you explain things.

Connect with the person
This concept of listing with your heart not only aligns you with the other person but allows you to understand what the other is saying by changing your perspective. You see, we tend to enter into all conversations with our opinions intact, but listening with your heart, you release your ego, your worldly views and self-directed agenda. With less baggage to carry with us, we tend to walk into conversations with an air of lightness that allows us to connect to one another with great ease and will make you more approachable.

You may want to ask yourself, when was the last time you can recall truly listening to someone? That is without offering any support, no lecturing, or interrupting with questions or past experiences or to submit a clever response. We are all guilty of this, and need to understand the benefits of truly listening.

I feel bad to say, I often used to find myself thinking of other things while my eyes would glaze over. I could not escape the internal racket; I was only pretending to listen. I only caught the important phrases, getting the gist of the topic but not absorbing the complete convo. So I was faking it! Yes, faking it! Hi I sometimes faked it!!! I would glance and nod only half listening which let's be honest... This is not listening!!!

I was so accustomed, to think that it would be rude to ask someone to wait to talk to me, or to talk at a different time.

But if I wasn't truly listening, heart listening is that not worse? What did I miss with all of this stress, and internal dialogue? In saying that, it makes me wonder... what was I missing then? What if this person could have imparted some imperative lesson that I was missing in my self-directed intermission? If we were to look at each person as a lesson then perhaps, we could expand our mindset. What does this person have to teach me? Remember, its not up to us to judge the book by the cover, or the car by its engine. It is our responsibility to listen long enough and intent enough to find out what the lesson is. It is an actual skill, one that can be easily acquired and absolutely be developed over time. This active art is not for the passive. You must be fully present to best appreciate the lesson, experience and offering that one has to offer you. Remember that listening is the most genuine form of flattery and compassion, which shows a deep connection and appreciation. Listening from the heart should expand your knowledge, give support to those who need it, is being respectful to those who are talking with compassion and empathy.

Here are a few examples of active heart listening:

Be fully present when the person is speaking to you

Ask relative questions, that do not import judgement or an opinion

Do no refer to your own examples, stick to their version and story.

Always respond from a place of love and compassion.

Release judgements and any expectations.

Remember its not about you at all
Always check in to what the person is stating.

Living an active and meaningful life starts with meaningful connections that usually stems from active heart listening. In this we have to choose to consciously slow down mentally, listen intently, give up our agendas and actively develop the capacity to focus our attention on others.

This in turn will develop a deep meaningful connection with others that will re-enforce the friendship, relationship and lessons we can learn from one another. At the root of listening with one's heart is desiring to lovingly appreciate what the person is saying and feeling to you. Approaching the other with sincere understanding gives the listener a glimpse into the sacred inner self of the other. This is not only a lesson but a gift in all that we do. Allow yourself to be mindful those who want to talk to us, and listen intently with your heart. Remember your heart is at your very core of your body. It is who we are, our hearts define us and rule our feelings. It is time to….. Feel with it, listen with it, love with it.

Questions

1. What makes you feel loved?

2. List 4 things you can do immediately that will start you on your self-love journey.

3. List 3 items that you plan to do to lead more of a heart-based life.

Era Six

─── >─I─<>─•─O─•─<>─I─< ───

Reinvest in Gratitude

Reinvest (verb)
re·invest ing (rĭ-vest′) tr.v. re·invested, re·invests

1. to invest again
2. to start, set in motion of investing,

Reinvesting in Gratitude

*J*t has been said that a grateful heart is a contented heart. A contented heart is a simple heart, and a simple heart leads to a simplified life. Gratitude opens the door to simplicity. This concept was always a bit odd for me as I at times. I mean I was always grateful for my life, and all of the blessings. But how can I be grateful for things that caused me pain, heartache and hardship? It was a part of growth that I was not too sure I wanted to grasp. I did however learn that this would be one of the most memorable and treasured gifts I could receive. You see to open your heart to pain as well as the good things opens you up to a very different king of life and understanding. A person who is grateful for all aspects of their lives, will care for them, enjoy them, and waste less energy seeking more. They will experience fulfillment in the gifts and hardships they experience rather than looking outside themselves for more. While living in gratitude is an acquired taste. Let's say that hearing "Well you know, you should be grateful for what you have," has got to be one of the most exasperating things you can hear when you're unhappy with your life. Especially if you're a teenager or have parents who like to drill this lesson home. However, it is actually, one of life's most valuable lessons that can ultimately work for you if applied properly. Recalibrating to learn to live in gratitude, can be learnt behavior, once you have let go of any yearning and bitterness about what it is that you don't have and train yourself to notice the things that you do. Here are a few ways to live in gratitude, each and every day for a positive outcome:

Express your gratitude-

In all aspects of your life when a friend, family member, colleague and/or client goes above and beyond, be sure to show or verbalize your appreciation in different ways. Get creative and show how much you care and appreciate them. Go to their office or treat them to lunch or a quick cup of coffee. Some companies establish a gratitude program or "Thank you Card" program that allows employees to thank their co-workers with a card, or gift certificate. A man I worked with many years ago used to hand out happy faced cookies. Some have merely brought in homemade treats or donuts to thank a team or coworkers. Trust me a donut or Timbit can go a long way!

Show respect for those around you-

Treat others with the same level of courtesy you expect to receive. Smiling, saying hello, showing kindness, exhibit patience and truly listen to listen and not to respond. Going for a coffee run, offer to bring back coffee for someone else in the office. Wash your coffee mug in the office kitchen rather than letting your dirty dishes sit in the sink. Hold the door, bring packages to your co-worker. Just doing the little things can make a world of difference.

Avoid complaining-

Becoming the negative nelly is not the type of status you want. When something terrible happens, and you know it will, it is inherently natural to want to complain about it. Becoming irritated, and impatient can negatively infuse your mood, verbiage and interactions with others. This will lead to others not wanting to work or interact with you either. Remember that each and every time you complain, you reinforce a negative state of mind without offering a solution to the problem. Alternatively, next time you feel frustrated, angry and update, take a few deep breaths and try focusing on something positive. *One quick tip I learned many moons ago was if someone has hurt, bothered or negatively impacted your day. Stop, Plot and Give. Stop the thoughts! Plot a positive good deed (Ha! you thought I was going to say something negative here!! LOL) and give it freely of yourself. Trust me, this will INSTANTLY change your vibe to that of a positive one!

Volunteer in your community-

There's a well-known secret among long-time volunteers, it is that any act of kindness does better for you than those who you are serving. Don't have much spare time? Donate business clothing to the local ladies' shelter, or take a therapy dog to a homeless shelter, read to children in the hospital or at the Retirement communities.

Remember, even if you don't have a lot of time to give, you can choose a volunteer opportunity that requires only an hour or two each month. Volunteering gives you something positive to focus on and is a great way to give back to the community at large.

The power of food

A powerful way to get a fast-track lesson in gratitude is to immerse yourself in the lives of others less fortunate than you. Try volunteering or donating food at a worthy organization that can provide some nourishment to those in need. You can assist in a soup kitchen to prepare meals at Christmas, help serving the homeless during holidays, or help with their food drives. It's always a good time to help especially when there are always mouths to feed. If you see a homeless person, buy them a coffee, or meal and merely smile and ask if they are hungry. Make the drop off and walk away knowing that you gave love with no strings attached.

Enjoy the big blue ball we call earth-

Joining a charity and clubs, to assist in clean up around the town, and/or donate money for churches, or shelters is always a great way to start. Help to improve your local environment, by picking up trash along the streets, or encourage proper recycling. Remember every little bit helps! It's time to be engaged and connected in your community. Set up a neighbor assistance network to help any elderly home owners around you who many need assistances with grass, snow or home repairs. Keeping the world around us clean and healthy is the best way to give gratitude not only to mother earth but to those we share this earth with.

Adopt a cause-

There are millions and millions of causes in this world that you now have so many to choose from. Find one or three that really speak to you and allow you to grow and become passionate about actively participating in. Join a cause that is near and dear to your family or perhaps those who are less fortunate than yourself. Get in touch with the key contacts and get started. Million Dollar Smiles, Feed It forward are just a few great causes that can institute change for a better community and a better world.

Be kind-

To help others less fortunate than you is an obligation not a choice. Whatever you do will come back to you, so why not make that a positive thing that will be seen and shared. If you see someone struggling with their groceries, lend a helping hand and help carry them or open the door for them. If you see a homeless person by giving them some cash if you can or buy them a meal will not only give goodness in this world but reset your thought process on others and not yourself. Try to always start your day with a great task of being kind.

Be generous-

By adopting a cause perhaps allocating a small percentage from your paycheck can go to a tiny village in need of a water source, or to adopting a child in another country, or buying a goat or cow for a village in Uganda. Pay for the education of girls, or to build a well in a poverty-stricken country. Remember money is a currency but it is also energy. To give it, is to receive it.

To reinvest in gratitude, we need to:
1. Intentionally choose it.
2. Count your blessings.
3. Stop focusing on what you don't have.
4. Embracing humility.
5. Looking to those in need.
6. Finding gratitude anywhere.

The benefits of living in gratitude are:

Gratitude makes us healthier and more resilient

Gratitude develops a spiritual and a far less materialistic perspective

Gratitude makes us happier, friendlier and definitely more optimistic

Gratitude makes us more likeable and deepens relationships

Gratitude strengthens our emotions and keeps our thoughts positive

Gratitude develops a positive personality and allows us to become more relaxed

Gratitude allows for better sleep patterns and over all more energy

Gratitude allows for better self-esteem, less envy and self-centered thoughts.

Gratitude ultimately allows for increased respect for others, and yourself.

Gratitude makes for better life management, increased networking and higher goal achievement in all career aspects.

Gratitude allows room for more respect, improved decision-making skills and overall increased productivity.

Gratitude has so much to offer, as once you start to truly embrace this way of life and invest in gratitude daily, you will see your life, your outlook and landscape change. It maybe subtle at first or may hit you all of a sudden. Remember you only need to change a small percentage and already your trajectory will change vastly. It is time to fully embrace life with a warm and happy heart. We can show gratitude for the blessings in our lives, for the love and valued assets but we must also be thankful for the painful lessons, the hurts and the pain. For it is in those experiences that allow for the most important lessons, and the validation that you were chosen for these special lessons. Please remember, that not everyone is chosen to be receiving of these experiences. It is time to get grateful!

Question:

What are 3 things you can give gratitude for?

What steps can you take today to include gratitude into your life?

List 3 past hurts that you have learned from.

Era Seven

—————— ⟩⊱⟨⟩⊶⊙⊷⟨⟩⊰⟨ ——————

Reclaiming.................... your beat

re·claim ing (rĭ-klām′) tr.v. re·claimed, re·claim·ing, re·claims

1. To resume possession of; take back:
2. Chiefly British To legally request what is due:
3. To require or deserve again:
4. To bring into or return to a suitable condition for use, as cultivation or habitation:

Reclaiming..................... your beat

For myself, music is my release, my refuge… it transports me directly to my happy place, or my LALA as I call it. Its my happy place that I can find bliss in an instant. For those that know me… finding my Lala is often reached by driving in my car with my favorite sunglasses, my tunes blaring and a bucket of sunshine shining hard upon my face. My music, can also bring me a myriad of emotions and can release me from any form of displeasure, stress, anger, anxiety and/or depression. It became my release…Ideally it brings me to a place of complete bliss within moments or just a few beats. For years I had found that when in a state of anger, it would take me hours to "calm down". This trait I learned over years of upbringing that I often found hard to shake. My process of unlearning this trait took me many years and often involved going for a walk, banging my fists on a wall, or simply going to the gym….as for myself having always worked out in a dojo feeling the physical pain was key regardless of the issue.

Years later, I realised that it was much more than that, and as easy as finding my zone to simply not allow the emotional stress point to rule my brain. As easy as it is to find my "state" in Lala it would be to not allow myself to go to the state of anger. By reclaiming your beat, you change your state and recalibrate it into a state that gives you what you need which is often calm, and resolve. You see humans are made up of 70% water, therefore any positive music, tunes, lyrics and verbiage allow your mind to change your state in a positive way. The benefits of listening to music is widely known and has been used in treatment for years for various illnesses. With the release of dopamines due to lowered blood pressure, not only improves muscle functionality but directly affects human RNA. This is demonstrated by reducing depression, anxiety and many types of chronic pain. You see humans are born with the ability to distinguish the difference between noise and various types of music and melodies. Slow music can reduce stress and calm the nerves while faster music and increase your heartbeat, blood pressure and breathing. Music supports us to feel strong emotions that has the power to move us and change our state of being. This in turn can reduce stress, ease pain and discomfort, improves memory, improves your mood, soothes the soul and lessen anxiety. So finding the type of music, tune or melody that calms your nerves and soothes your soul is key. It is also imperative to find what type of music plugs you in. What allows you to get in flow or claim your beat.

Many have asked me what does reclaiming your beat actually mean? To some it is recalibrating to a better state with deep breathing, if could be meditations, singing or simply going for a walk. Not everyone needs to listen to their favorite tune or start driving their car to find their "Lala". Now, I have not met anyone who does not like music. So, for most is it simply the action of finding what can recalibrate your state but for some it is the beat of your heard. Ok, I am not getting emotionally deep here…. I mean by simply focusing on your mental state and finding your beat and setting your pause button on hold.

You can do this by the following:

Listening to your favorite music
Focus on your breathing
Focus on your heart beating
Meditation (guided or not)
Exercise
Running or walking
Take time to re-calibrate

When listening to music, I feel at peace, I feel passionate and I feel reborn all at the same time.

For some close friends, I know they truly live for music, and for some it is their sacred place. Music affects us in so many different ways, as it is one soulful medium that reaches each of us all regardless of race, gender or religion yet varies on its effect on each and every one of us.

For some very close to me… music resides within them. It is in their veins; it beats within their heart and resides within their soul. It lifts them higher than life itself and transports them to their special place of bliss that allows them to reside within their flow. Imagine how diffcrent life would be if we could just infuse music in all that we do. If music changes your mood, and uplifts us, then finding it in our everyday life is imperative. Well with the introduction of the modern cell phone we can now listen to music almost at any time listing to almost anything at anytime. Auh-mazing!!! How relevant and how inspiring! Having played piano for 4 years, clarinet for 2 and violin for 5 I have a very eclectic musical taste, that ranges from classical, rock, reggae to country and pop. So, for myself, listening to different types of music, is all dependant on my mood, my state and that days activity. I suggest to always to try something new.

Never say never and expose yourself to all types of music and allow it to bring you to the place the artist navigates your path to. Allow yourself to be released to a place of happy or your own version of LALA. Remember it can become your refuge, it will bring a smile and perhaps a clear path to your happy place.

Finding your Lala!

Infants, and small children can find their happy place within seconds. So why is that as we grow older that it takes us such a long time to find our state of happy? Do you ever notice how quickly a child will get up and start dancing? Or pop their head or move and shake to a beat regardless if they ever heard the song before? It is innate as a human that we all have an inner beat. Now don't get me wrong, I don't mean that everyone can dance but everyone can find their beat by learning what their body is telling them. For some it is soft classical music that allows them to glide and move to a slow methodic groove. Yet other will tap, bang or drum on almost anything around them. Its amazing to me how certain things in your life just click when you have reclaimed your beat. It has been proved in many scientific studies that music and moods are inherently linked. Studies continue to support and uncover how these each influence each other and occur at a neural level. Studies prove that the music we listen to engages a wide range of neurobiological systems that affect our psychology. It is all too easy today to easily be upset or rise to anger, yet finding your beat is so key to recalibrate your stated while keeping yourself grounded and in a good state of flow. Ideally your mindset or perception can be on demand by choosing music that provokes a specific emotional response or state of flow. We can use music as a tool when you work out or in your daily life exactly the same way. Our emotional response to music is very individual and dependant on moods and perception. Now not all happy songs are universally apparent as being uplifting or are guaranteed to put you in a good mood, however finding that right song is a combination of soothing and uplifting or something cathartic and powerful dependant on your mood.

If you can target the mindset you want to snap into and then choose the music to tap into this conscious state-of-mind by entering a sub-conscious level. Neuroscientists have found that music enters our nervous system through the auditory brainstem and this also causes the cerebellum to 'light up' on a brain scan, and is the most powerful neurobiological tools to change your mindset, behavior or state. The human body is made to move and can be moved by music as the mind relates to the beat of the tune. So finding your power song or anthem is key to recalibrating your state and finding your flow. Some choose songs that have a particular beat while others choose a slower song with a strong verbal or emotional resonance that can supercharge you in moments. Note that having a few power songs or anthems are key that you may reserve some for certain times when you need a particular trigger that cues a specific state of mind or alter-ego of peak performance on demand. As I write this chapter I am listening to my favorite soulful singer and mentor Jai Jadeesh, with one of my all-time favorite songs…. I am Thine. It engulfs the room with a slow elegance that transforms my surroundings into a place of tranquillity. It enlightens my mood and allows my mind to be transformed into a serine place in mere moments to allow me to reach the proper state to write. This is my bliss. This allows me to reclaim my beat and transform my mood, my state and my inner love within mere moments. I had the amazing pleasure of meeting Jai about a year ago during her world tour and her one day stop to Toronto. I was invited by a dear friend of mine Andrea who said it was a definite must come event as she knew Jai personally. Oh my was she so right!! Listening and watching Jai sing her songs in a small downtown yoga studio uplifted me to such a place where as I looked around I could clearly see how this song so transformed the whole audience. Some slayed to the music lost in their own flow, others intently watched Jai as she sang, smiling and voicing the worlds to her song. All artists have their flow, they own their beat and as they sing, they allow you to travel along with them to be transported to their sacred creative place thru the beats and words of their songs. As I watched Jai sing, I felt her voice raise, and I could see the moments where her eyes close and she was singing in a place of complete happy or LALA. She was the song. She owned her beat and resided in her place of bliss. She has now cultivated a life around what brings her life, brings her bliss, each and everyday. In this I find my peace, tears run from eyes to my face and onto my laptop, as I feel myself, transported to this place of solitude, peace and purpose. As I write/type I feel myself being lifted with renewed purpose and contentment. I am thine ...... Finding your beat is to listen within and finding the rhythm within you. Finding your inner beat or rhythm is to listen to all types of music and allow you self to feel. To truly feel what your inner voice tells you. Experiment and try out new music, tunes and musicians to offer a variety to your selection. You will be amazed with what you find out about yourself. Set the intention to find out what lights you up, and gives you life. What transforms you and uplifts you from a dark place and allows you to soar higher than before. Some of my personal favorites would reflect my musicality from Lindsey Sterling-to Satnam Kaur – Grace and Deva Premal – Embrace. Look for music that truly transports you to a different place and allow it to move you there and infuse it in your day each and every day. From listening on your way to or from work, to listening during the day or on your break. Find the time to bring in the light, the music and allow the beat to move you inside and out. Whether you are an athlete or not you can use music to find your flow and maintain an upbeat momentum and rise above the dark and angry moments. This will keep you centered and happy reclaiming the happiness each and every day. Similar to an athlete finding their zone to best preform it is also to prove that finding what gives you life and purpose also gives us the best unique chemical endorphins to make us happy.

One of my nearest and dearest of friends, Chan who is in my inner circle gave me the best description of finding my beat or my LALA. In countless conversations thru the years we have addressed so many topics of happiness, some trauma and sensitive issues and thru it all she has always enforced that living to my own beat, my flow, my groove is always what is best for me. Topics, timelines and expectation are never good when given by others. Living for other people's standards will also never give you the peace you crave. Regardless, finding your beat thru your music allows ourselves to connect to our inner peace and flow. It is in this connection that our brain can resolve what is truly best for us. Chan would always ask me "does this feel good for you? Allowing me to truly find my flow, and if the situation and/or decision was correct for me. Never pushing nor pulling me in any particular direction. This unconditional support allowed me to learn that this was the support I needed to truly connect with my inner intentions without weighing what others expected. You see our gut instincts are usually correct.

This has always proven itself to be not only correct but the rule to live by. As pushing or pulling does not work unless you are in flow with your own intention. Finding your beat is maintaining that system within your life for a balance and happy life. Now, not everyone has an amazing and inspiration woman like my "Chan" in their lives, but all you need is to trusting your own instinct. You see your gut instinct is your body, your mind, and your unconscious mind giving you a hint and/or suggestion that something is off. This is truly finding your beat and living in your flow.

Keys to finding your beat:

Make a list of songs that totally light you up

Pull together a play list on your phone, or tablet so you can recharge at anytime.

Ensure to interject music though-out your day

Make a list of daily things that are imperative for you to maintain your flow

Question:

What is your beat? Find your jam!

What music lights you up and transcends your mood and state?

What song just completely releases you of all strain, despair and heartache?

List out 5 songs that affect you:

1. calms you –

2. uplifts you –

3. gives you momentum?

4. Allows a moment for pause-

5. Brings you to your happy place-

Era Eight

Re-launch your best you

Relaunch ing*vb* (*tr*)

1. to launch again
2. to start, set in motion, or make available again

Re-launching your best you

*H*ow do you relaunch the best version of you? Great question!

Very much like unveiling a new hair cut or new outfit. By investing the time and energy into yourself it will always yield a gift of improvement, self awareness and pride in oneself. Relaunching the best version of yourself is part of that process and is daunting for most, but although all of us want it, not many actually take the time to complete this in their life time.

It is the human condition to want to stride for the betterment of ourselves, it is by the conditioning of pride and shame that we often get sidelined and try not invest in other things with a faster thru any change. We all crave to be the best you, or best version of yourself that you can possibly be. Striving for more, to learn, to unlearn, to better yourself, always starts from the inside out. Its within the process of silence and looking within that we all commence to work on ourselves. So, doing "the work" is imperative to knowing yourself and what you can fix. There also needs to be a defining element of truth. What is the truth, you ask? Again, great question... Its digging deep within oneself, to find, and coming to accept the dark ugly and twisted elements of ourselves that we often keep hidden away from others and ourselves for years. It is the deep-seated hurt, angry or ugly truth of ourselves that we don't want others to see. The question is, why hold on to these when we can deal with them release and be free? Fantastic question, but it is the answer that most do not want to address. Remember, don't ask the question that you are not ready to hear the answer to. Right??? Wow what a concept. This is not a new nor earth shattering thought pattern yet it eludes most. A person who wants to relaunch themselves needs to understand, accept and truly want to change. Its like joining a gym but actually going! The yearning to learn, must expand in all facets of your life. to want more than this life can give at the moment. To understand that it is all there for the asking. To want more than what the norm or society offers you or advises. It is to be bold, to live large and to be as awesome as you can be. How amazing to want something that no one else has ever think of. When you look at all aspects of your life you need to look at all internal and external elements in order to truly make any lasting changes. We can all talk about losing weight, changing our wardrobe, our jobs, and our hair. But it's the need hard seated uglies that I talking about the hard stuff that most of us are challenged to change without a hard pressed DDD (Drop Dead Date).Most of us will wait for an important occasion, a medical issue, or simply having your face against a wall in order to make these changes.

My suggestion is to write them down. List all of the actions you can take to start these changes. Some can be small steps, some can be large and scary steps (you may have to work up to those!) But all in all, by writing them down we give weight and relevance to them. By listing the steps (even the small ones) gives you momentum to this goal. Keep the list in a visible place and make sure to look at it and reference it as much as possible. It must stay relevant in your life to uncover the best you. Relaunching the best you, is to live life to the outmost and correctly identify what needs to be corrected and changed and set those intentions into action. Taking care of yourself is paramount both mentally and physically. This means to eat right, sleep enough and give time to re-connect with yourself. If not, what are we working for anyways? We are all here to live and eventually die. Yes, I said die! Unless your immortal, none of us come out of here alive so to live the best version of yourself and take care of your mind, your body and your spirit.

Secondly, you must fully understand that in this amazing world of ours, there are many things we have control over but we don't have absolute control over everything. It is in this key point that seems to derail most. If we remember that we can not control everything, and everyone, then the very acceptance of what we can not control allows us to truly live in the moment. Learn to accept what we can not control and change that what we can. Live life as life presents itself. I call this Living Freely. Case in point: if you have a person in your life, be it in your work life, home life or personal life that is doing things purposely to upset you or irritate you. The normal mind set would be to get upset and think that this person was doing this on purpose. Now don't get me wrong. Some people will do things to personally irritate you. (we all have them!) My response to that is send them love, clearly, they need it. ☺ Whaaa???

For those who truthfully don't have a clue, there is probably a lack of understanding of what they need to do. Most of us walk thru life without keeping everyone else's opinion in mind. If this person, is upsetting you, understand that YOU can not change them. They are the only person that can do this. Step away! Know that you only have control over yourself, what you do, what you think, and ultimately how you affect others around you. Send them love (yes its actually outlined in Chapter 5.. or send them gratitude Chapter 6) to fully release them. That person at the office that seems to always get under your skin doesn't really get up every day, and plot revenge on how best to irritate you! LOL. They are simply navigating thru life the best way they can not truly knowing how certain behaviors affect those around them. Trust me, I know these people too. It is best to gently remind them if certain behaviors bank on the ridiculous or can I say rude… but it is not up to us to reprimand others for their behaviors, unless they are to harm others. Now do some people not know when to blow their nose until they drip on your desk, or to not read their emails out loud? Perhaps they never knew cutting their nails in public is not accepted or cutting people off when answering a question, they asked was not a lesson yet learned. However, and I mean a large HOWEVER....... (sorry had to hold for a dramatic effect as I don't have any music interlude to fully embrace my thoughts here!) This person is probably navigating thru their own insecurities that does not enable them to properly ask and answer in the normal context. Here I thought it was me, yet a person's response is most likely a visible condition of other deep-seated issues of their own. Don't take ownership of their issues or build resentment or anger. Simply stop and walk away. Remember, we all live within our own minds and will color our landscape differently than most. Not all of us live in a colorful and happy world. Some simply don't know. We can remind them and gently (yes, I said very gently) assist but ultimately it is best for most if you send them on their way with love (they need it) and gratitude for giving us the opportunity to learn from their behavior. Odd concept I know but it is vital to truly live the best version of yourself. Understanding and accepting ourselves is also understanding and accepting others as well. You see in pulling in all that we have read thru, tried, learned and unlearned in this process assists us to grow in a divine and natural way.

Here is one of my favorite quotes on control.

"Incredible change happens in your life when you decide to take control of what you do have power over instead of craving control over what you don't."

— Steve Maraboli,

A dear friend of mine Laurin often said to me.... What made you happy today? I would often shrug and say... hmmmm not sure! What??? He would respond. Even when I had the most horrible day, his response was to console me, wasn't in changing what was bugging me, or to tell me to stop, as he had no control over that. He would simply drop off a happy face cookie. He would leave them on my desk, my monitor, or in my office. It was his way of changing my perspective to get the best version of ME out. Wow! What a concept. He would often give out happy face cookies to all that helped him on a large project or simply if you had a bad day, or more importantly if he had a bad day. This got me to thinking... even when he was upset, irritated or angry he never showed it.

He changed what he had control over and spread happiness and gratitude all around him as this was the best version of himself. Now he is not an author or self-help guru... but this lesson has truly shock me to my very core. I have spent many many years traveling the globe researching spirituality, different religions and talking to many acclaimed mentors. But this lesson had hit home, all of what I have been conditioned to unlearn in the past 5 to 7 years. Now we are all works in progress and Laurin will be the first to tell you that he is not perfect but it is his acceptance and smile that always seems to leave you feeling happy regardless if you agree with him or not. Now that to me is one of the best examples you can find of people being the best version of yourself. For some it can take years, decades, for others they can leave this earth without really finding this for themselves. I feel that we owe it to ourselves, and those around us and ultimately our species to navigate thru this life to find the best version of ourselves. It is in that ability to see far outside of ourselves that we can truly grow and merge as a species. Now I was lucky enough to not only find some amazing people along my travels to help me learn this, (not everyone can have a version of Laurin) but to recognize and accept this lesson. I was once told that if you ask then the universe shall conspire to bring this to you. How so? Well, let's say I asked for that. Plain and simple. In this one life we have to live we should all aspire to live it to the best of our abilities and if and where possible aspire others to do the same each and every day. ☺ I now am inspired each and everyday to do things effortlessly never expecting a thank you or fan-fair. I simply go on my merry way, doing things without being asked, completing things for others and simply smile and walk away... the feeling is truly immeasurable. It warms my heart with such gratitude to see the sparkle in their eyes and smile on their face. Not don't get me wrong, there will be the odd person who will ask you why are you doing that? Or try to question you to death about what your true motives are. These are the people most affected. The cynics beware... we are only out to please, and god forbit make you smile! ☺ Having the innate ability to change our perspective and our minds to affect ourselves and our environment is such a wide range of ways is truly a immeasurable talent and valued attribute. As this will benefit us in so many ways in all aspects of our lives. Our perspective relies on us entirely, changing it and opening up ourselves is genuinely easy once we have learned the why and how. Giving flame to what lights you up-I am often asked what lights me up. For me its making people smile. Bringing in flowers from my garden to those who love the surprise of flowers on their desk. For purging, books I have read and donating to our office to share in the beautiful thing that it is to read. It is to take a day off and help build a playground or simply take a day off to spend a day with a close friend in need. If can be almost anything that you can do for others that fills up your cup or lights you up. Go visit a friend who is moving and help out. I also love learning and reading new books, new concepts and travel, so I have found that those attracted to my energy also love to hear what I have learned, the adventures of my travel as well as any new courses or book I have read. Remember to expand of ourselves and your interests we often expand those around us. There is a huge world of people out there that can not only expand your thought patterns but also expand your ability to learn and reach new levels in our quest for knowledge as well. Learning was not meant to be taken alone. Expand your consciousness and allow others to enjoy your journey. Take in what you have learned and find out what enlightens you. Expand on that and watch it multiply into other positive variations of itself. Like watching a garden grow, allow yourself to water what you seed and watch what happens. Positive attracts positive.

For the most successful people in the world, success didn't come overnight and did not drop in their lap. Success was also not instant and in only one aspect of their lives. Most had to work hard at becoming the best person that they could possibly be. Here are a few ways to unleash your awesome.

Focus on what you want to become-

A good starting point is to work out what it is that you are looking for in life. Set yourself some intentions and think about where you would like to be in ten, fifteen or twenty years from now and you will see a plan start to formulate. It is the base of all plans is to know what to focus on.

Why so serious-

The Joker said it best... "Why so serious?" I simply LOVE this phrase and even have a mug to remind me. By laughing at yourself once in a while, regardless of what happens is the key to longevity. If something bad happens, recognize the problem and try your best to fix it. If it's not going to affects you in two years, don't sweat it. Forget about it and move on.

Believe in yourself-

This is difficult for most but regardless of what others thinks, whatever your dreams, the only one person will make them come true and that is you! By recognizing your own gifts and capacities you can believe in yourself and thrive. Remember, you are much more capable than you think you are.

Stop and smell the grass-

So truly what's the rush? As long as you're there, you might as well make the most of it especially if you won't ever be there again! Have fun in the moment and don't be rushing around in a frenzied pace all the time. If you see something you like, spend as much time as possible there! Life isn't about rushing around and being stressed. You are you're not being the best person that you can possibly be if you are constantly stressed. Calm down, slow down and really stop and smell the beauty in the grass, trees, coffee and perhaps a nicely baked scone!

Gain inspiration-

Take a look around and find others that genuinely have the traits and personality you want to be. No need to copy but truly encompass the trait your best identify with and make it your own. Staying true to yourself, above all is key but remember you can learn from almost anyone around you. Another great venue would be to read biographies and/or historical text looking at the brave and talent souls from our history is always inspirational and great resource.

Surround yourself with positive people-

Remove what does not serve you and try to not let those negative people get you down. There will always be someone who will be happy to shatter your dreams or give you a Poopoo platter of negative meats to eat! Ensure to surround yourself with only positive people and happy people that you admire and some their positivity will run off on you.

Get organized-

Getting organized, purging, and decluttering ensures that nothing will allow you to get distracted. This also clears the way for newness and gives your "clutter" a new home. Whatever your ambitions and/or your goals are, the more focused you are to achieving them, the easier it will be. Plan for your yearly purging and don't forget your local causes that rely on donations to assist those in need. This is a great way to give new life to items that are lost in your home and release you from the clutter.

Nurture your dreams-

Don't ignore your dreams, focus on them, plan them and follow the path. Every single day, you must try something that will take you a step closer to becoming the person that you want to be and to nurture your dream. It likely won't happen overnight, but remember the dream is also part of the journey.... so be patient, persistent and passionate

Get plugged in and well read-

Reading in general tends to inspire most but reading inspirational books and vowing to never stop learning is the truest form of being awesome. You see in this you remain open to new ideas. Reading will become such a habit and crucial part of your life that it will fuel your newest desires and keep you motivated and tuned in. Have knowledge on what's going on around you...watch the news or read the newspaper to read up on a certain topic. Also, to read and write well would mean you would be increasing your vocabulary. It's always good to be intelligent and knowledgeable about things and you never know when that information will become useful!

Be adventurous-
Find a hobby. Discover what makes you tick! Perhaps singing, playing an instrument, writing, learning, exercise, dance, collecting things, making movies, scrap booking, animals, hiking. Find what you truly enjoy and fills you with passion and get out there! If you love to paint, take painting lessons or practice every day! If you like dance join a dance group and meet new people. If you like the outdoors, try hiking, then try new paths, set out some new adventures and perhaps try hiking in Peru in the sacred lands of the Incas at Macchu Picchu or thru the beautiful lands of Chile! Think large and be adventurous.

Practice makes perfect-
Whatever your goal and what you aspire to be, you will need to practice, practice and repeat. To build and improve on your natural talents is always a bit hard at first but remember that mistakes are a part of learning. Practice is key and perhaps finding someone who already is on this road will and can assist you as a possible running buddy!

Find and elevate your style and make it your own-
Being you, makes you the best version of yourself, so wearing unique clothes that fit your style is key. Try to add something to standard clothing and make it your signature look. Be different and don't care what others think about this. Don't be afraid to be a little out there; you might set a good example for others who wish to be true to themselves. Don't care what other people think of you, as they'll forget about that girl wearing the crazy unique outfit in less than 5 minutes anyway. Some unique accessories and clothes are: feather earrings, beanie hats, long or unique necklaces, friendship or bangle bracelets, arm bracelets, sharp rings, etc. Find outfits that you like that fit your style and

that you personally like, and most of all have fun with it! Just be yourself and be the best you can be at it!

Jump out of your comfort zone-

If you tell yourself that you can't, then you won't, if your too old, you will be older tomorrow. So get going! Be prepared to take on new challenges and try new things. Think outside the box and identify what you want to do and work towards it. Think outside of your normal parameters as becoming a better person doesn't mean changing who you are, but it does mean pushing at the boundaries a bit harder. Are you wanting to sky dive? Pungee jumping perhaps? Ok, Ok this is not for everyone but you know what I mean.

Yesterday is gone ...Start today-

Many of us think that we could be a better person if... we had more time, if you had more money... Simply start today. they could be a better Stop the promising and do something about it today. Making a start allows your trajectory to change even by the smallest percentage. You have to start some time, so decide for that to be today. Get up and go!

Smile at all costs-

Smile often, laugh often. A fantastic way to make yourself feel good is to genuinely smile. If you smile regularly, people will smile back and this happiness will come back tenfold. When you smile, you feel warm inside, and that feels good. If you not in a good mood and are seriously trying to be happy then go out and buy a few smile cookies (or donuts for that matter) and distribute to your office, or co-workers. This will be sure to set the people around you in a collective smile!

Keys to relaunching yourself:

Make a list of things that light you up

Male a list of the changes you want to implement daily.

Set up notes of positive mantras as re-enforcements

Make a point to appreciate those around you.

Journal what positive accomplishments you have been able to complete.

Questions:

What have I learned and want to expand upon?

What is my passion or mission in life?

List 5 things I have always wanted to do to unleash the best version of me.

1)

2)

3)

4)

5)

How can you action these today?

Quotes To Review:

One life is all we have and we live it as we believe in living it.
But to sacrifice what you are and to live without belief, that
is a fate more terrible than dying.

~Joan of Arc

Fate Whispers to the warrior "You cannot withstand the storm"
and the warrior whispers back..." I am the storm".

You are a warrior of the light. Heal yourself, Fight for love,
Save the earth.

Warriors are not born, and they are not made....
Warriors create themselves through trial and error, pain
and suffering, and their ability to conquer their own faults....

A Warrior of Light values a child's eyes because they are able
to look at the world without bitterness. When he wants to find
out if the person beside him is worthy of his trust, he tries to
see him as a child would.

Warriors of light are not perfect. Their beauty lies in accepting this fact and still desiring to grow and learn. ~ Paulo Coelho

Before commencing battle, the warrior of light opens his heart and ask God to inspire him. ~ Paulo Coelho

Warrior's Creed
Honesty-Always be true to myself, stand for virtue. Humility-Acknowledge weakness, never flaunt my strength. Control of Power-Never abuse that which I have learned, always be aware. Courage-Face my fears, acknowledge them stand tall, facing danger. Concentration-Invoke the strength of body, mind and spirit. Endurance-Focus and training is my stability, strong and powerful is my body, my spirit is my drive.

References / Sources

"What is EFT?"
The Origins and Background
http://www.theenergytherapycentre.co.uk/eft-explained.htm

"What Is Tapping and How Does It Work?"
https://www.tappingsolutionfoundation.org/howdoesitwork/

"Creating Positive Intentions"
https://www.gohealthclub.co.za › creating-positive-intentions

"THE COMPASSIONATE GARDENER: A MINISTRY
OF HOPE MEANING & HISTORY OF MALA BEADS"
by Deborah King
https://thecompassionategardener.wordpress.com/2015/07/07/
    meaning-history-of-mala-beads/

"5 Spiritual Benefits from Journaling (God's Spiritual
Cross-trainer)"
By Charles Stone
https://charlesstone.com/5-spiritual-benefits-journaling-gods-
    spiritual-cross-trainer/

"The Healing Benefits of Grounding the Human Body"
By Marty Zucker, Gaetan Chevalier, PhD, Clint Ober, Paul J.
Mills, Deepak Chopra, MD
https://www.huffpost.com/entry/the-healing-
benefits-of-grounding-the-human-body_b_
592c585be4b07d848fdc058a

"THE ART OF GROUNDING & 30 WAYS TO DO IT"
Aware
https://awaremeditationapp.com/the-art-of-grounding-30-
ways-to-do-it/

"A Distance Learning Diploma Course of 12 Lessons"
Crystal Healing Course
https://naturalhealthcourses.com/courses/crystal-healing/

"The Free Dictionary"
by Farlex

"Lessons of Life-Relationships"
by DR. LALITAA
https://www.youtube.com/watch?v=m1IQCz9XjAY

"5 Simple Ways to Express Gratitude Every Day"
by Jacqueline Whitmore
https://www.entrepreneur.com/article/235785

Suggested Resources

Reading
Spirit Junkie – Gabrielle Bernstein
The Universe Has Your Back – Gabrielle Bernstein
Alchemy – Paolo Coelho
Grow a new Body – Dr. Alberto Villodo
Crazy Sexy Juice – Kris Carr
Radical Self Love – Gala Darling
Course of Miracles –Foundation of Inner Peace
Universe has your back – Gabrielle Bernstein
Divine Compensation-Marianne Williamson
Warrior of Light – Paolo Coelho
Return to Love – Marianne Williamson
The 5am Club-Robin Sharma
Everything is Figureoutable – Marie Forleo

Music
Jai Jadeesh – I am thine
Jai Jadeesh – in dreams
Eivor – Trollabundin
Eivor-I Tokuni
Julia Elena-108 Gayatri Mantra

Julia Elena – Mantras of Light Album
Snatam Kaur – Ra Ma Sa Da
Snatam Kaur – Long time sunshine
Lindsey Sterling – Transcendence
Deva Premal – The Essence Album
Deva Premal – Calma e Tranquilidade

Apps
Headspace Meditation & Sleep
Deep Meditation: Relaxation & Sleep
Mindfulness Coach
Let's Meditate: Guided Meditation
365 Gratitude Journal & Mindfulness Coach
Self Healing – The Wellness Platform

Charities
Million Dollar smiles –Anna Lopez
Feed it Forward.ca-Jagger Gordan
Plan International

Shared Thoughts

J started this book at a time my path was so unclear, so picking up this book you were also probably unclear as to what you were looking for. Or what you truly needed to expand your thoughts and direction. For myself, the name and concept came to me in a dream with little direction and guidance, like an uncharted map but a desire to travel. As I wrote, my words came freely and my path to become clearer. It was never my plan to expand nor change to this level or degree but something inside changed. Something inside that was yearning for change, wanting and craved more was ignited. This build a passion, a mission and a inner sense of purpose that I always knew was possible within me. From the moment that that book fell on my head I knew I was in for the ride of my life, I just never suspected to this degree. You see, I asked for it. I asked the universe to become a better version of myself and I wanted it and my mind was seeking it unbeknownst to me.

Deep down I knew that something larger than myself was leading me. This path was all part of the process, and this book was a way to help others. So you reading this book is all part of my dream. It was in writing this book that my life, my spiritual path and my personal journey became crystal clear and shone brightly especially in the darkness that surrounded me. It is with this that I felt engaged and my true inner strength began to appear. You see, they say you write about what you want to learn. Tears well up in my eyes as I write this, knowing that many of you also feel this purpose, but don't know what to do, or where to start. Your path is also part of my path, we are all connected and support in each others dreams and aspirations. What I say to most is look within and allow the universe to guide you. Ask for assistance for the greater good with love in your heart. Once you do, all will fall into place. You see in life we look amongst the branches for connection, yet it is within the roots that we need to truly connect with one another, looking past the regular similarities or even differences. I started this journey of writing ideally for myself and the passion and lessons, that I was seeking yet, I found all within my own heart. The lessons were all internal. I realise now that I wrote this book for you the reader. To assist you on your path and may these words give you momentum, spark your passion and assist you during your travels. Allow this book to accompany you on your journey. Learn and write your notes, agree to disagree, or agree if you feel aligned to but continue the journey, truly live and continue to seek and ask questions. Let it nourish your soul, ignite your mind, and inspire you to greatness. Become the best version of you.

Be Bold

Live Large

And unleash your awesome

Acknowledgements

To my kids, you are both truly my life, my inspiration and endeared part of my soul. Nicolas and Victoria, for your unwavering love and support, the laughter, and for the unique lessons that aligned me to become a better parent, a better person and a more conscious human being. You keep me sane and drove me insane all at the same time. I am so thankful for your roles in my life and how imperative the lessons are that we impart together. Thank you and I love you to the moon and back.

To my aunt Amelia who has always been my best friend, my confidant, my mom, my mentor, my sister and clearly the loudest cheerleader. Thank you for allowing me to grow on this path and never having to explain, yet completely understand my crazy, without judgement.

To my family, Zio, Mark, Laura, Jojobean, Jamie, Matteo, and Maya for your unconditional support and love in all of times of happiness, joy and pain we remain solid.

To my dearest inner circle:

Chan R. for unconditionally supporting me, thru the chaos, the turmoil and the tragedy all while showing me a new direction and path of a better soulful life. Your entrance into my life, so pivotal and potent timing. Your energy, your love and unconditional support never waivered, yet so vastly inspiring. You are my rock and my inspiration of what a beautiful soul is and can be I humbly thank you

To Riri – Rita C. – my Bister, my BFF, and soul-mate, and sister, who simply gets me with few words for the majority of my life. There are no words to properly express the love that radiates between us and for this I am eternally thank you. My life changed early that cold March day at George Brown College, and I am forever thankful for your connection and love in all aspects of my crazy life and ambitions. Our love and appreciation expanded with our families and the beautiful memories and bonds we have made. Our lives, our familys forever bonded. I thank you, I love you…..my sister.

To all of the Cuni's – Sam, GP, Julia, Michael, Juliana, Shania, and the entire Cuni, Geraci, Guzzo, Volpe and Arruda clans who have become my family and my heart. I love you and thank you.

To Angela S, Zak L and Noreen K. my spiritual mentors who not only presented me with a different vision of the world, but enlightened my understanding, my spiritual growth and my humanity. It is thru your eyes that I have truly grown to understand and unlearn all that the world has to offer. You are all inspirational mentors and teachers… and as a student I am humbly grateful.

Iman, and Missy you are both my inspiration and my light of glee that you both show and inspire me each and everyday that thru the greatest tragedy there are lessons, laughter and growth in us all. I thank you.

April T. my soul sister, my love and happiness guru.... Such amazing times traveling the world, you have shown me how effortlessly friendship can be, and how kindness knows no boundaries. You are my cheerleader and I am so very happy we traveled this path around the globe and thru our growth together.

Nicole VK and Renee M. thank you for holding me up, and standing by me when I was too weak to talk and process, I owe my sanity to you both and will be forever grateful. Single moms everywhere deserve this type of tribe to feel one and whole again.

Cstarr – Thru our travels your sisterhood and dynamic presence who radiates the true meaning of sisterhood. Thank you for the lessons and allow me to grow without opinion. Thank you giving me the room for true growth.

Kathie S.-my BFF, my original SRB-spiritual running buddy and soul mate. I thank you for not only showing up but for voicing the hard truth even when I didn't want to hear it. For making me accountable when I know it wasn't easy and it necessary. For stepping up and stepping back without words, and simply just knowing. I love you.

Shey, Armin, Arnaam, Darrius, and Raji thank you for reminding me that staying honest, transparent and with integrity. I thank you for allowing me to grow in my gift and giving me the soft resting place of your support to learn and the validation of what I was learning.

Laurin S – thank you for reminding me that living my path, is better served with a smile and integrity. It is not how you start, but always how you finish the race by how many people you positively affected in the time you were here. I thank you for the lessons Thank you!

Lisa Y. My unicorn and garden fairy. I thank you for helping me make sense of this path and that if doesn't matter how old, how young and how inexperienced you are, we can conquer all that is set upon us with happiness, grace and success. Keep dancing, I love you!

Annamaria L, Debbie W, Wanda L,
Oh, my magical three. I met you so many years ago and thru the years you have all shown me the strength it takes to be a genuine and loving person in all that you do. Your generosity, your love, support and advice thru the hardest of times your support shown bright showing me the way home. For this thank you each humbly and from my whole heart.

Shelly R, Oh the stories we have. The lessons and hard truths we negotiated thru. I humbly thank you for being my steadfast friend, a confident, my cheerleader and my coffee/breakfast buddy thru all of the turmoil, happiness, kids and joy.

A special thank you to my spirit angel Kimberly, you were a definite Earth Angel, who now guides us all from heaven. You gave me the courage to become the Spirit Warrior I aspired to be, even when I was uncertain. You gave me hope, you supported me with your words and inspirational words. You believed in me when I was a mess, still finding my way.

I thank you for the motivational portrait you did of me as a Spirit Warrior and our many enlightened chats. I thank you; I love you and I miss you.........each and every day. Stay in light Kimberly Hopkins Bliss.

Thank you to my Peru team and The Four Winds; Michela, Molly, Jennifer M, Rose, Chelsea, Marie-Therese, Karen, Marie-Clara, Manose, Marcela and Alberto for assisting and allowing my growth to expand and release me beyond what I knew was even possible. Our travel to the sacred valley will forever remain in my heart, in my soul and deep in my mind. I will forever be changed from our time together.

To the amazing Medicine Women of Los Lobos in Chile. Thank you, Marcela, Lisa, Fernanda, Holly, Angela, Laura, Mina, Rachel, Ariel, Barbara, Ashley, Kielly, Ariel, Manuela, Anne, Alli, Nicole, Georgia, Skye, Wendy, Therese, Charlene, Martina, Michelle, Lynne, Robin, Emma-June and Luisclara. A'Ho

I thank you for supporting me and holding space in all of the many lessons and experiences we navigated thru in our growth and expansion. Our time together was powerful, and everchanging, our bond everlasting. Thank you to Machi, the mountains and beautiful lands of Pachemama and how they now fuel me each and everyday.

In Gratitude
Thank you with all of my heart, for those who supported me, and pushed me along my path.

Thank you with all of my gratitude to those who broke me, for those wounds that healed brought lessons I could never have imagined and the wisdom I am thankful for.

Thank you for those who said I couldn't and forced my conviction to push forward.

I thank you God and the universe for guiding me thru my path, I stand before you with much love and gratitude for making my life a challenge and worth the lessons given to me. For without those, I would not be the person I am today. I am today more enlightened, living my passion and mission as if it was my last day.

Thankyou, thankyou, thankyou.

Namaste
~R
Rita Aldo Rasi

After Thoughts

As my journey continues, I realised that although this book took a lot longer than I anticipated, it was a journey well spent. I would not have changed a thing. This project was completely handled outside of my comfort zone and was a complete labor of love and caring. A project of self-love, self-discovery, and awakening mind, body and soul. I guess it was truly part of my unlearning path as this was so different from my normal day to day life. I finished this book in awe of the freedom and knowledge it has given me. Although, it took many years later than I originally anticipated, I am fully empowered by the power of this path. You see, like the path of awakening it is not on our schedule, all plans, shattered. We as humans all set up guidelines, timelines and with pre-conceived expectations of how we think things unfold, how it will be revealed. This path was pushing me to uncharted territories with many twists, turns and turbulence, and none of which I was truly ready for. You see, this path of unlearning is a path of the unknown, as the universe is in the driver's seat with the GPS on turbo. This path of writing, was also my path of awakening and I realize now, that this was organically going to take as much time which was required. No less, no more and right on que. When it was ready to be completed then it would be revealed. Many people close to me would repeatedly ask when this book is ever going to be completed, and my response was always the same.............. soon! You see, it was in writing this book, in each chapter that I studied, understood and fully incorporated all that was written. I lived and experienced every single lesson, every word and each understanding, like waves of realizations that penetrated into my consciousness. It was a living path that organically lead me all while keeping me on my toes. It was a study of a few years, processing and documenting each phase that this book transitioned into what it is today.

The universc also sent me many people to re-enforce my path and what I was learning and compiling in each chapter. The picture of the cover I held close, and my journal always in my bag, and my favorite pencil/pen. My journey was clearly destined, with each phase taking me thru the lessons I had to work thru. This book has been my path for the past almost 3+ years. It has been in my every thought, and consumed my mind for so many minutes, hours, days, weeks and years.... it has carried me thru all of my learning, it consumed me at times and I simply loved it....i reveled in it. I leave it now, like a great friend who has held onto my hand the whole way...... sharing my successes, my losses, each lesson, and my breakthroughs of heart wrenching realizations and downloads. Yet, as daunting as this was.... Its scary to finally let go of. I pray that this book will also carry you and assist you in and on your path to whatever it is that you are looking for, learning or unlearning, and yearning to bring into your life. This is now YOUR path.... It is all in your journey that everything will unfold to what it is to needed to be. For each of us, it will commence from the time you many not even remember. My hope is that your journey will open you up and this book, will assist you to manifest its lessons to everyone in a very different way. Remember this journey is yours, not meant to be the same for anyone. Namaste, my dear reader....At the end of this book I send you many blessings and my sincere gratitude that you allowed me and my humble words to join you on your sacred path.

I thank you; I love you; I support you and I wish you well.

Printed in the United States
By Bookmasters